Stock Options Trading

Learn to Understand How it Works and What Pitfalls You Should Avoid as a Beginner. You'll Learn How Top Investors Lower their Cost Basis by Using Stock Options

Jim Livermore

Table of Contents

Introduction

Welcome to stock option trading. My name is Jim Livermore, and I have made a living trading stock. In this book, I am going to teach you what I have learned over the years the hard way, but things that have completely transformed my financial situation.

You see, I was a lot worse off than many readers are today when I began my stock trading career. I was living in poverty but managed to scrape together $5,000 overtime. I knew that I had to change my situation and improve my life, so I began investing in stocks. Slowly at first, so that I would not put much money at risk at any one time.

I had some wins and some losses, but gradually I learned the ropes of stock trading. Pretty soon, I was getting more consistent in earning profits. After a period of a few years, I was able to turn my initial investment of $5,000 into $100,000!

Now obviously I cannot guarantee that you will have the same success. However, I will teach you what I have learned, and this will help you start off in the right direction. I also want to emphasize that yes, it is possible for anyone to earn profits trading stocks!

In this book, we are going, to begin with a review of stock options. For clarity, this is not trading options on the derivatives market. Rather, I am going to be discussing stock options offered by employers. This is an opportunity to build wealth that many people overlook or fail to take full advantage of.

After this, we will discuss the long-term value investing philosophy promoted by Warren Buffett, so that you can learn a relatively safe and surefire way to build wealth. We will learn how to be successful trading stocks in good markets and bad so that you can build wealth over the long term no matter what happens.

After we learn the basic philosophy behind successful investing, we will learn about how to become an independent stock trader. I will guide you through the process of setting up a brokerage account, how to trade stocks, and mitigating risks. We will also cover the basics of how the stock market works for those who are not educated in this.

Then we will talk more about employee stock options in detail.

For the rest of the book, we will talk about many of the important issues surrounding investing. This will include the issues surrounding ETFs, and whether or not they are better than buying individual stocks. We will also talk about different metrics used to determine whether or not a stock is a good investment and what to look for. We will also cover IPO investing and tax issues surrounding stocks.

I wish all readers the greatest success in trading stocks, and hope that you can start building wealth the way that I did!

Keep in mind that past performance is not a guarantee of future success, and that the information provided in this book is not to be taken as financial advice because it is offered for educational purposes only, and not being aware of any readers specific financial situation I am not in a position to offer anyone advice. If you have questions or need advice for your situation please contact your own financial advisor.

Thanks!

Chapter 1: An Overview of Employee Stock Options

If you have the opportunity to invest in stock options at your place of employment, this is not something that you should pass up. Many people fail to take full advantage of this because they don't fully understand what it is about and what it can do for them, while others prefer to have cash in the here and now. This is a mistake for most people. Any type of ownership stake that you can get in a corporation, including your own place of employment, is something that can help you build significant wealth over time. In fact, it is one of the best ways to build wealth over time short of you starting your own business. And even if you were to start your own business, there are very good odds that your business is going to fail! But if you are working for a corporation that has become large enough to offer you stock options, this is a sign of a stable company that is growing, and that has a lot of potentials. For some, this can represent an unprecedented opportunity to grow wealth.

Of course, as an investor, diversity is always the number one rule that you should keep in mind. So don't make the mistake of thinking that I am suggesting you let your entire future ride on your own companies stock options. I am not suggesting that at all. Rather, if you have the opportunity to invest through employee stock options, this is just one more part of your toolkit that you should use in order to increase your own personal wealth and secure your financial future.

In this chapter, we will introduce the basics behind the concept.

What are Employee Stock Options?

Many companies offer employee stock option plans. These are offers of stock to employees. The offer will give the employee the right to buy shares of stock in the company. They are called stock options because the purchase is optional; it is a right on behalf of the employee and not an obligation or requirement.

The employee stock options are going to be time-limited. Typically, these will have an expiration date that will be a given number of years in the future. The company will offer the options to employees at a certain price, and if the company is publicly traded, this price can be compared favorably to the market price of the stock in many cases. The terminology that is used is whether or not the employee stock options are "in the money" or "out of the money." If the price that is offered to the employee is lower than the price that the employee would have to pay buying the shares on the open market, they say that the stock options are "in the money." They are "out of the money" otherwise. Whether or not this is the case can be important if the employee is running out of time to exercise their right to buy the stocks. It will also depend on the financial health of the company and its long term prospects. Of course, as an employee of the company, you might have a better idea than a member of the general public as to what the long term prospects of the company may be since you might know about products that are in development by the firm that can have a large impact later.

In many cases, stock options can be worth a lot of money to employees. They can represent an opportunity to build and grow your own wealth as a part of a larger self-directed investment plan.

Employee stock options come with many specific characteristics, properties, and requirements. Knowing what these are will help you navigate the world of employee stock options and help you decide how to move forward with your investment plans.

Granting of Employee Stock Options

Employee stock options, technically speaking, are derivative options similar to those used to trade on the options market, but they are given to employees and management executives at the company. However, there are some differences. First of all, employee stock options often come with an expiration date that can be years in the future, giving the employee a significant amount of time to decide whether or not to buy the stock. Second, the options are granted to employees, that is given by the company to the employees as a part of their compensation plan. In the case of employee stock options, the other party in the transaction is the company itself. Employee stock options are often issued by publicly traded companies, which is very helpful when trying to determine the true value of the options since the employee will be able to compare the offered price to the current market price. However, employee stock options can also be offered by private companies. In this case, determining the real value of the stock might be difficult, but the employee will be able to weigh different factors to determine whether or not it is worth buying the stock. For example, if the company is growing or has major products in development, and this is attracting a large amount of investment, it is probably worth it to the employee to invest in the stock. This will enable the employee to not only benefit from being employed at the company, but they can also benefit from growing with the company as well.

At a later date, if the company ends up going public, this can be a tremendous opportunity for employees to become wealthy overnight. If you are working for a private company that you believe will go public in the future, and you have the opportunity to buy stock in the company, this is something that you must do. When the company goes public, oftentimes the price of the shares will go up by a large amount compared to what you have paid for them. You can sell your shares and acquire large amounts of cash. Consider that when this has happened in the past, companies like Microsoft minted many new millionaires. Of course, few people are lucky enough to work for a company like Microsoft, but you don't have to work at a company that big and successful to benefit from an IPO.

Employee options are *call* options, which gives the holder of the option the right to buy shares of stock at a specific price. No matter what time period a company chooses to use, the options come with a defined expiration date. If the employee chooses not to buy the stock, and they expire, the employee is out of luck. You have to exercise your right to buy stock on or before the expiration date. If you don't do so, they say that the options expire worthlessly. The bottom line is that if this happens, you have passed up your opportunity to own shares of stock in the company, through this method.

In the case of employee stock options, the company will offer them a favorable price per share to the employee. Therefore it is usually advantageous to exercise the options. Of course, if the company is publicly traded, the price of the stock can drop in the marketplace, meaning that it won't be favorable for you to exercise your rights to the shares. That is because you must pay the price specified in the option for the shares of stock. So in the event that the price of the stock declines, the employee would be in a situation where it is not worth it for them to exercise the options.

When you are given stock options by the company as a part of your compensation, we say that the company has granted you the stock options. This is because you are not required to buy them yourself on an options exchange. In short, the company is giving you options in lieu of higher pay, and members of the public would have to buy these options on the exchange.

However, you should be aware that you cannot trade the options. While a member of the general public can buy options on the exchanges and trade them to earn profits, you cannot trade the options themselves if they have been granted by the company. The only way that an employee can benefit financially from these types of options is by exercising them to buy shares of stock in the company.

Vesting Date

Stock options that are issued to employees come with a vesting date. The vesting date places a limitation as to when you are able to exercise your options. The vesting date will be at some point in the future. So you will be granted the stock options, but you will not be able to exercise them before the vesting date arrives. The vesting date is something that will be written into the options contract. Ordinary stock options that are traded on the exchanges do not have vesting dates, and American type options can be exercised at any date on or before the options expire. That is not the case with employee stock options that are issued by the company they work for. In part, a vesting date may be incorporated so that the company gets a bit of assurance that the employee will work at the company for a given period of time before the employee decides to leave and work somewhere else.

For example, suppose that you start a new job at Acme Widgets Corporation on June 1, 2020. As a part of your compensation plan, Acme might offer you options to buy 1,000 shares in the company. Hoping that they can use the prospect of owning stock in the company to keep you interested in working there, they may have a vesting date of January 2, 2021. That means that you could not exercise the options until January 2, 2021. This provides some incentives for you to keep working for the company.

When the vesting date has passed, your stock grants are "vested." That means that you then have the right to exercise (see below).

Many companies have a 90-day rule. That is, if you are vested and you choose to retire or leave the company, you have 90 days within which you can buy the stock. If you are vested and leave your place of employment, if you don't buy the stocks within 90 days then after that you have given up your rights to buy the stock using the options. This means that if you wanted to buy the stock after 90 days, you would have to buy shares on the open market and at the market price. Of course, if it was a private company, then you would no longer be able to buy the shares.

Grant Price

The grant price is the price specified in the options contract that you can use in order to buy shares of stock from the company. The grant price plays the same role as the strike price does for a publicly-traded options contract. This means that no matter what the market price of the stock is, the employee has the right to buy shares of stock at the grant price if they have become vested (that is the vesting date has arrived, and the options have not expired). Companies do this in order to offer a benefit to their employees. Of course, if the company is publicly traded, they have no control over the market price, and it may not always be in a favorable position for those who are interested in exercising their stock options.

Vesting Equally

If you hear from your employer that the stock options are vested equally, this will also be accompanied by some time frame. Let's say that it is five years, starting with year one. If you are granted 100,000 shares of stock, at year 1 if the shares are vested equally, then 20,000 shares of stock will be vested at the end of year 1. Then at the end of year 2, 20,000 more shares will be vested, and so on. This will give you the opportunity to exercise your options in pieces along the way.

You may also hear the term "cliff vesting." If stock options are cliff vested for one year, that means you have to stay working at the company for at least one year before you can exercise the options.

Exercising Employee Stock Options

Exercising employee stock options simply means that you purchase the stock. When this is done, that means that the options contract itself is voided, and in its place, you get the shares of stock.

If the company is traded publicly, you are going to want to keep an eye on the market price of the stock. This is going to help you determine whether or not owning stock in the company at a price offered in the stock options, makes it worth exercising them. For example, if you are working for a company whose shares are trading at $14 a share on the open market, but the company has offered you shares of stock at $20 a share, it is not worth exercising the options. This is the out of the money condition. In options trading, out of the money options are never exercised for obvious reasons.

How would you get in this situation? At the time you started your employment, the company shares might have been trading at $30 a share, but the company had a vesting date many months or years in the future, so you were not able to exercise the options while the market price was higher than the price set in the options.

Companies seek to offer the stock at a discount, so in many cases, you will find that it is beneficial to exercise your rights and buy the shares. For example, maybe the employer issued stock options at $20 share, but by the time of the vesting date, the stock is trading at $40 a share. As a result, you have the opportunity to benefit from owning the shares.

Employee Stock Options – Terminology

Let's go through some of the terminology associated with employee stock options so that all readers are familiar with and understand them. There are just a few things that you need to be aware of when it comes to employee stock options. These include:

- Issue Date: That is just the date that the options were issued to the employee or "granted."
- Grant price: If the employee decides to buy the stock, the stock must be sold to the employee at this price.
- Market price: This is the price of the stock on the open market if the company is publicly traded.
- Vesting date: The employee cannot exercise the stock options before this date.
- Expiration date: If the employee has not exercised the options by this date, the options expire, and the employee loses the benefit. If the company is publicly traded, they can still buy shares of stock, but they are on their own.

Stock Price and Private Companies

Although private companies are not traded on stock markets, and so there is technically no "market price," the company has a valuation that comes from the revenues and profits of the company. Often privately traded companies inflate their value based on the future prospect that a product the company is developing or just starting to sell may have. As a result of fluctuating or increasing revenues and possible profits, the value that shares of stock in the company may have will change, even if there was some arbitrariness that came with associating them with a specific value in the first place. As a result, employees can still benefit from having the shares available at a discount as to what the company would charge outside investors to pay for shares in the company.

Should you put your all in the company?

One mistake that employees often make is putting all of their investments in the company that they work for. In the old days, this may have made sense. But today only someone who was ignorant of the principles of good investing would do such a thing. One of the most important rules when it comes to investing is diversification. This rule still applies even if you are given the opportunity of employee stock options. So, in this case, you should definitely not put all of your investment dollars into the company even though you work there. At most, you should probably put 10% of the money you have for investing purposes for the company. If the company is publicly traded, this won't be an issue, because you will be able to sell your shares on the market. Then you can use the profits from the transaction (assuming that the options were in the money at the time you exercised them – and there would not be a good reason to exercise them if they were not), in order to buy shares in other stocks or funds.

Some Common Mistakes

It's easy to make mistakes when it comes to employee stock options. For one, most people are not truly financially literate. In fact, we could probably say that most people are not financially literate at all. To make matters worse, stock options go beyond stocks themselves, and so people can have a hard time understanding the process and what is really involved.

In the old days, people would work for a company for a long time period, often for their entire working lives. That is no longer the case. Today, most people are going to change jobs multiple times before they retire.

As a result, if you are granted employee stock options, one of the things that you need to be aware of is what the policies are in the plan if you leave the company. Not knowing these important bits of information is something that is a major mistake when it comes to employer stock options.

When you are offered employee stock options, you need to familiarize yourself with the policies that are in place with regard to what happens if you leave the company before exercising the options. You will need to know what happens if you are fired (most likely the options would be null and void) if you are laid off, if you retire, or if you find a job elsewhere. As we mentioned above, in most cases, assuming that you are leaving the company on decent terms and were not fired, there will be a 90 day period where you can still exercise the options. This is given because the options were a part of your compensation plan as an employee. Therefore, if you leave the company but you haven't exercised the options, you need to find out right away if the vesting date has passed. If it is a public company, you need to be keeping an eye on the market price of the stock so that you exercise your options when they are in the money. Do not exercise out of the money employee stock options unless you are looking at a stock that you are interested in investing in over the long term.

Know the tax laws

When it comes to investing, you need to know the tax laws when it comes to any financial transaction. You might find that you are in a position of owing a large amount of taxes if you acquire shares of stock and decide to sell them right away. We are going to discuss the issues surrounding taxes and investing in chapter 10 of this book.

Know the vesting period

Employers want to give incentive for employees to stay at the company, so the vesting period is not going to be a short time frame. They are interested in keeping you there (that is, giving you the incentive to stay) for at least a year. Most companies that have employee stock options have a vesting period of 1 to 4 years. Remember that the options are probably going to expire in 90 days at any time you leave the company. So you need to have these dates firm within your mind. The typical expiration date for a company offering stock options is 5-10 years after the vesting date. So if you are planning on staying at the company for a while, you will have a significant time frame over which to monitor the stock and only exercise your rights to buy the shares when the stock goes in the money, if it is not in the money when the vesting date arrives.

Are Stock Options for You?

Whether or not stock options are right for your particular situation is something that is going to depend on your financial state and where the company is along its growth cycle. If you are working for a public company that has good prices offered in their stock option plans relative to the market price, then it is a no brainer to buy the shares, at least for the purpose of selling them in order to make a profit. If you are anxious to move to another job or retire, and the market price makes the options out of the money, then it is not worth exercising or worrying about your employee stock options.

Private Company Stock Options

If you are working for a private company, the picture can get more complicated. Many times, you will find that a private company is offering stock options as compensation because they are not able to pay salaries that compete at market prices. If the company is a startup, this can provide employees with a chance to directly share in the company's massive growth should it occur. In a private company, however, employee stock options may not be liquid for a long time, if ever. There is not a public market for stocks held in private companies, and so it may be very difficult for employees to actually convert their shares of stock into cash. If the company is acquired by an outside buyer, then this would be one such opportunity, but it may require waiting around a long period of time for something of this nature to happen. The second major possibility is that the company will go public with an IPO, and once the company is public as an employee with shares of stock, you can then sell them on the open market.

How an IPO Can Turn Employee Stock Options Into Large Amounts of Money

There is no doubt that you have heard the stories about employees at startup companies that went public and became millionaires. The process could work something like this. You get a job at a new company, that has a lot of promise because it will disrupt some market. The company is short on cash in the beginning, and so it will offer you 50,000 shares of stock through a stock option plan with a grant price of $0.50 a share. So it would cost you $25,000 to buy all the shares.

You work for the company for five years, and then it becomes public. After the IPO, the stock price is $14 a share.

Your expiration date is still a year into the future. You could exercise the options now, which would certainly be a smart move. So let's say that you decide to do that, so you have to spend $25,000 to buy the shares at $0.50 a share. At the time you joined the company when it was just starting, $0.50 a share might have been all the shares were objectively worth. And remember that with stock options, the price that is paid for the shares must be the grant price, no matter what the market price of the shares happens to be. That is the rule that is legally in force until the expiration date. Of course, the company appreciates the loyalty of the employees that have stuck with the company to this point and so it won't be unhappy with this situation.

However, now that the stock is publicly traded you can immediately turn around and sell your shares for $14 a share. You can sell some or all of the shares. That is entirely up to you. If you decided to sell all of the shares, you would earn $700,000 from the sale, for a net profit (ignoring taxes) of $675,000.

You could also wait and see. If the company has good prospects, in a year it might be trading for $30 a share, and then you could sell your shares for $1.5 million. Alternatively, you could hold onto the shares for the long term. It's entirely up to you, and nobody can force you to sell the shares.

Chapter 2: The Oracle of Omaha

In this chapter, we are going to discuss the solid principles of long term investing. These are the principles followed by and promoted by Warren Buffett and others. This is why we are titling the chapter "Oracle of Omaha."

The basic fundamentals behind this type of investing are focused on investing in companies for the purpose of building long term wealth. This is not a get rich quick scheme, but rather a process centered on picking solid investments that you can stick with for many years in order to build wealth for the future. At some point down the road, you can start cashing out your stock for a profit. The reason this works is that if you are careful about what companies you invest in, and you are getting out of bad investments when then signals are there, you are going to find that you have gained considerable wealth over the years.

Over the long term, while there are many ups and downs in between including recessions that can sometimes be extremely severe, stocks appreciate in value. Of course, not every stock is going to appreciate in value, because many companies fail, or at least fail to hold onto their market share and don't realize the potential they once had. But many companies will grow in size with the economy, and usually, this growth will outpace inflation. At the end of a ten, twenty, or thirty-year time span, the value of the stocks that you hold will appreciate in value by a large amount.

Investors who follow this type of plan can then take advantage of that wealth of appreciation by slowly converting their holdings into cash. You can use this cash to buy the things you've always dreamed of, to travel, or simply to maintain the kind of middle-class lifestyle that you are used to.

Fundamentals and their role in long term investing

The first thing we need to think about when considering long term investing is the fact that we are looking for companies that we can stick with for many years, if not decades. That means that you have to get a full understanding of where the company stands at the time you are investing, and you also need to keep up with the state of the company as time goes on.

A large part of this is a periodic evaluation of the company's financial statements. You need to know how the company's profit and revenues are trending, and you should evaluate this information on an annual basis to keep up with their fortunes. Of course, one bad year doesn't indicate that you should abandon the investment, you are looking to see how the company is faring over time. Three and five-year trends are important to look at.

The Intelligent Investor

Warren Buffett's style of investing begins with a concept promoted in the book *Intelligent Investor* written by Benjamin Graham. In the book, Graham promoted the idea of finding value stocks. These are stocks that are priced below the true value of the company. Then, according to Graham, you would hold these stocks until they rise to their true value.

The basic idea behind a value stock is that the company is trading at a share price that is below where it should be. Each company in the stock market has an *intrinsic value*. This is the value you would give the company based on its financials, that is what are the income and cash flows for the company, and how is the company growing year to year. You can use intrinsic value to estimate the price of a stock.

There is not a specific formula to use. Rather, you would compare the intrinsic value of the company to other companies in the same sector or industry. Then you would compare the stock price of the company. If the company has a low stock price relative to other companies in its sector that are performing at a similar or lower level financially, then you know the stock of the company is underpriced, making it a value stock.

There are other factors that cannot be quantified that would be looked at in order to determine whether or not a stock is a value stock or not. For example, you would look at the research and development going on at the firm. If a low priced pharmaceutical stock, for example, is for a company that is working on a breakthrough diabetes drug that is expected to be approved by the FDA and be on the market within five years, then you know the company has intrinsic value that isn't being priced into the stock.

Another factor that can be examined is the management team. If the company has a solid management team that is well respected in its industry, but the stock of the company has a relatively low price, this can be a reason to consider it a value stock.

Fundamental Analysis in Detail

The main way that professional investors determine whether or not a stock is underpriced, priced just right, or overpriced, is to use fundamental analysis. Fundamental analysis is not the same as technical analysis. Investors that are long term investors don't use technical analysis at all. Technical analysis is a tool that is used to guess which direction the stock price is going to move over the course of a few hours, days, or maybe weeks. If you hear anyone talking about technical analysis, then they are not investing, they are speculating. And they are certainly not following the methods used by Warren Buffett. Technical analysis is only looking at the behavior of prices of the stock over short term periods, and it doesn't matter at all what the company is, who is managing it, or what the company's long term plans are.

Fundamental analysis, in many ways, is the exact opposite of technical analysis. When you are doing a fundamental analysis of a company, you are not at all concerned with the short term price movements of the company. You don't care how it's moving day to day, or even over the course of weeks. In fact, you don't even care what the share price is, other than looking for stocks that are undervalued relative to what the intrinsic value of the company would indicate the stock should be priced at.

The first thing that is considered in fundamental analysis is the state of the sector from an economic perspective. While we are often concerned with recessions and bear markets, individual sectors can have their own recessions or downturns while the rest of the economy is doing well, or vice versa. For example, you could focus on the oil and natural gas industry. In the early days after the recession that followed the 2008 financial crash, the industry began to see the widespread use of fracking. As a result, while the rest of the economy was either declining or barely beginning to recover, the oil and natural gas industry was undergoing the beginnings of its own economic boom.

Those kinds of relative differences, economically speaking, between sectors are something that needs to be considered first, so that you would have an idea of what a good price for a stock would be. In the example above, you would expect the value of energy stocks related to oil and natural gas to be priced above average for companies with the same underlying cash flows.

The main factors to consider with fundamental analysis are revenue, earnings, profit margins, and the annual return on the stock price. You will also want to know how much debt the company is carrying. The most important factor here is going to be the growth or decline in the amount of debt. Just like looking at the financial health of a household or individual, a company that is showing an increasing debt load is probably not a good investment. However, if a company is decreasing their debt load, even if they have a large amount of absolute debt, that could be a sign that the company may be a good investment going forward if they are showing improvement in other numbers as well.

There are three financial statements, all publicly available, that you should look at when considering the fundamental analysis of a company. These include the income statement, the balance sheet, and cash flow. Let's examine each in turn.

Income Statement

The income statement provides important information about revenue and profits for the company. You can examine income statements annually and by quarter. An investor will be looking for trends in the income statements. For example, is gross profit increasing each year, or stagnant or declining? A stock that is underpriced relative to its competitors in the same sector but that shows an increasing gross profit for the past 3-5 years might be a stock that is a valuable investment. When looking at quarterly data, you should look at the same quarter for each year, in order to account for seasonal differences in economic activity related to the company.

There are many other things to look at on the income statement besides gross profit and revenues. For example, you should check the operating income or loss. But don't check it blindly. Of course, the general hope would be to see steadily increasing operating income. You certainly don't want to see operating losses – in general. However, the future potential of the company might figure when looking at these numbers. Research and development is an important operating expense, and as we cited above, if you were looking at a pharmaceutical company and it had a declining operating income because it had massively increased spending on research and development, then the operating loss may not be an important factor to consider. We know that spending now on research and development is definitely something that can pay off later for a company. Other companies might be on the cutting edge and have a potentially disruptive product that could mean the stock is going to have a lot more value down the road as compared to its current status. For example, Tesla has large operating losses, but many investors are big believers in the future promise that electric cars hold, and so they may be willing to put up with operating losses now, in the belief that Tesla will experience future growth later due to the advantages it has holding potentially disruptive technology as an asset.

At the bottom of the income statement, you will find net income, and also net income applicable to common shares. These values are going to be something to look at, and again you want to look at trends. If the company shows steadily increasing net income year to year, over the course of 3-5 years, this is an indication that this could be a value stock.

Balance Sheet

The next financial statement that you want to look at when doing the fundamental analysis of the company is the balance sheet. The balance sheet is something that you can use to see the assets and liabilities of the company. You will want to compare the total current assets and total current liabilities. While you are going to want to look at total current liabilities and see what the trends are, be sure to also compare total current liabilities to total current assets on a percentage basis. If the company has increased debt loads year to year, but it's growing so much that as a percentage of total assets the debt is decreasing, then this is still a company that is financially healthy. You will also want to check long term debt and accounts payable.

At the bottom of the balance sheet for a publicly-traded company, you are going to find information about stocks. Here you will find the total number of shares that are available, along with the retained earnings of the company and treasury stock. If a company is paying out dividends (not all companies do), retained earnings are going to be the amount of net income that the company keeps for itself or retains. The reason that they will retain some of the net income is so that they have profits on hand that can be reinvested into the company. This may be done in the form of increasing spending on research and development, or building new manufacturing plants or hiring more workers. If a company pays no dividends, then it's going to keep all of its net income as retained earnings.The capital surplus of the company will also be listed here. This is the net worth of the company that is not classified as retained earnings.

Treasury stock is shares of stock that the company is keeping for itself and not currently offering to the public. It could, for example, be shares of stock that it has "bought back." The shares are then kept in the treasury of the company as an asset. It could later offer them to the public.

Cash Flow

The last financial statement that you want to examine when doing fundamental analysis is called cash flow. The first line of a cash flow statement is the net income of the company. Ideally, you will want to see the net income increased year over year. You will also want to compare the net income of the company to the net income of similar companies in the same sector that have higher stock prices. For readers who are not clear on the definition of net income, this would be total sales minus the cost of goods sold. The costs will include all expenses such as administrative expenses, depreciation, marketing, taxes, and so forth.

On a cash flow statement, you will find some information on operating expenses below the net income listing. So you will see depreciation and some other items. Investment activities by the company will also be listed.

At the bottom of the cash flow statement, you will see any information available on dividends paid by the company and net borrowings. If the company is not paying dividends, this line will be left blank. Net borrowings are the total borrowed funds used for the operating expenses of the business.

Why the company's value is important

For the value investor, or for that matter any investor, the price paid for a stock is going to be determining the long term return on investment. Of course, you are still taking a risk by investing in a value stock. Even though the financial statements may be indicating that the stock should be priced higher than it is, the market may not come to agree with that assessment, and the price might not rise as expected. Also sometimes stocks that you would consider overpriced relative to their underlying value may continue to increase in price because of hype or expectations. Emotion often plays a role in the pricing of stocks, and high-tech stocks, for example, are going to generate a lot more emotion and excitement than a utility stock, to take an extreme example. That can be true even if the high tech company is not even earning profits. A stock in a more slow-moving industry could be earning a lot more profits, but investors will be drawn to the high tech stock because of the perception that it will earn high profits in the future.

Nonetheless, you are playing the odds of probability in the stock market. We can confidently say that the probability is going to favor value stocks increasing in share price over time if they have good fundamentals.

One way you can quantify value is by looking at the Shiller PE10 valuation of a stock. This will give you an idea as to the risk of the investment and the implied long term returns. A low Shiller PE10 value means that the investment is a lower risk investment and that it's likely to have a higher rate of return in the future. Conversely, a higher Shiller PE10 value means the investment is higher risk, and it is more likely to have lower rates of return in the future. The Shiller PE10 ratio averages the data over a 10 year period and accounts for inflation. By using the Shiller PE10 ratio, you can average out temporary fluctuations that occur over time. For example, you can account for a year or two of unusual earnings by the company, or average out stock market crashes like the 2008 financial crisis or boom times as well. So the Shiller PE10 will give you an averaged price to earnings ratio that can be used to more accurately interpret the price to earnings ratio of the company and its value. A low value indicates that the company is a good investment. You can compare values between companies, sectors, or by using the S & P 500 index. You can also look up important information such as the distribution of companies by Shiller PE ratio for a sector.

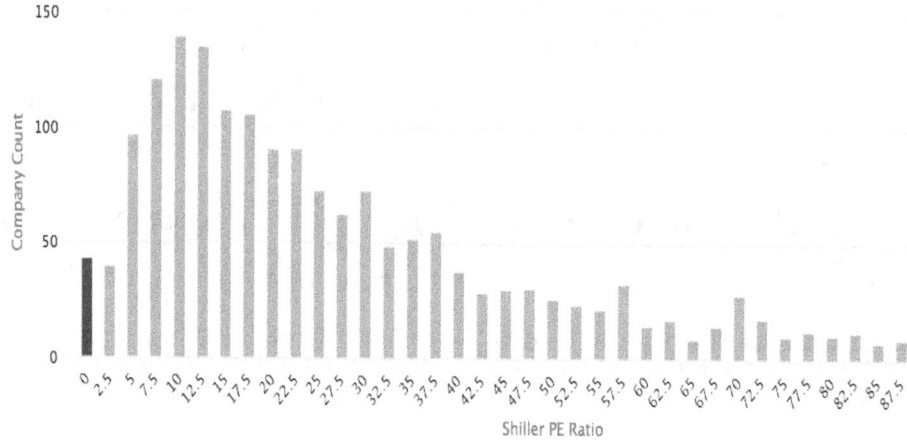

Shiller PE Ratio for Tech/Social Media sector, calculated by Guru.com

Inefficient Pricing

You will often hear the term "inefficient pricing" when we are discussing value investing. The idea behind this concept is that the pricing for certain companies in the market is often inefficient, that is not representing the true value of the company behind the stock. So you should not be looking at the stock price alone in order to determine the true value of the company, and the idea behind inefficient pricing is that over the long term, the market is going to revert back to the true valuation of the company.

The Warren Buffett Strategy

With the ideas of fundamental analysis clear in our minds and what to look for, we can discuss the strategy used by Warren Buffett in picking investments. This is a good strategy to use if you are looking to hold onto stocks for the long term. That is, you are looking to hold onto your investments for at least a 5 year period, but more typically one to three decades of time.

Of course, things will change as time goes on. Although a stock might be a solid value investment for the next 3-5 years, that does not guarantee that it is going to be a solid value investment for the next 10 or 20 years. So once a year, when companies release their 4th quarter earnings, and you are able to completely review their data for the previous year to see how things are going, you can evaluate whether or not the company is still worth investing in. You are not required to hold all of your investments if they are not working out, and you should be looking for better investments if you find stocks in your portfolio are not performing as hoped.

Now let's consider the most important principles that Warren Buffett follows in his investing.

Stick with Your Investments and Don't Panic

One of the biggest enemies of investors is emotion. You see nearly everyone following the lemmings over a cliff, whether it's buying up an overpriced stock or getting out of the stock market at the slightest downturn. The two emotions that people experience in the stock market that are destructive are greed and panic. When it comes to greed, people will buy up stocks hoping to strike it rich, preferably over the short term. It is completely natural to experience this emotion. However, you should not give in to it because it's a destructive emotion when it comes to investing. You will find yourself paying too much for stocks, often buying up shares at peak prices before they drop back down. Remember that although it happens occasionally, in the vast majority of cases nobody is going to get rich quick. Building wealth is something that takes time, usually a long time. Therefore you should be methodical in your stock purchases. If you are feeling some kind of adrenaline rush, or a sense that you have to buy up stocks NOW in order to get the growth in value that you are expecting, these are red flags that indicate you should take a step back.

Of course, the worst impulse when it comes to the stock market is selling off your shares in a panic, when there is a bear market or a given stock is declining. People do this all the time, getting out of the market when there is a short term downtrend so they can supposedly preserve their cash. This is the true lemming behavior, and it's a major contributing factor to crashing stock prices. Warren Buffett is not someone who is going to dump his shares over a short term fluctuation. Remember that you are in your investments for the long term, which means for decades, or at a minimum at least five years. A recession is going to be a mere blip over the course of 10 or more years, and often even over five years of time. Even during the Great Depression, stocks rallied and began increasing in 1933. And as we know, the Great Depression was an anomaly. It could happen again, but the chances of it happening are low. Beyond the Great Depression, most recessions are short-lived, and the markets often begin their recovery before the economy fights its way out of a recession. If you are investing with a time horizon of ten or twenty years, a downturn that lasts 9 months to two years at the most is not going to be important in the end. So avoid the impulse to sell and hold onto your investments instead.

People who panic and exit the markets, only to get back in later, often end up having to buy back shares at higher prices.
In short, Warren Buffett advises that investors never sell when they panic.

Invest like it's your business

Warren Buffett tells investors that they should act like they are buying the company. All too often, people invest in their gut feelings. They get excited about say Amazon or Netflix, and so throw all their money into these stocks, without looking at the fundamental analysis. If you were going to buy a local business to generate income for yourself, would you invest in that fashion? No, you would not. If you were buying a business, you would pour over its financial statements with a fine-tooth comb. You'd want to know what the plans are for the future and what has been done to take the company in that direction. You'd want to have a clear picture of any debt that the company had taken on and so forth. Warren Buffett advises that you look at stocks in exactly the same way. Even though you are only buying into a small fraction of the company with the stocks that you buy, you are counting on this company providing for your future wealth and retirement. So you should treat it as if you were investing in it for the long haul.

Invest in Quality

Warren Buffett aims to invest in quality companies. Ideally, he would like to find value stocks that are underpriced, but he is also willing to pay the fair market value for a company that is a quality investment. Something that naïve investors fall for that is often promoted by internet gurus looking to sell people "systems" is investing in cheap stocks, because they are cheap. This is not something that fits into the Warren Buffett investment strategy. You should absolutely stay away from penny stocks, and Warren Buffett is not someone who would put his money in low-quality companies just because they have cheap stock prices. It's important to note that the goal of investment using this method is to find companies that have solid fundamentals but relatively low stock prices, or companies with solid fundamentals that also have fair stock prices. You are not looking to invest in a company that is in poor shape and has mediocre prospects going forward, just because it has a cheap stock price and you would hope to earn profits because the price might bump up at some point. That is a game played by gamblers. If you are using the Warren Buffet investment strategy, you are not going to be gambling with your investments.

Look for Competitive Advantages

Seek out companies that have important competitive advantages that will help the company beat out its competition over the long run. This can include new product development, established branding, or the ownership of strategic assets like important patents. Using the example of a pharmaceutical company again, if there is a company that holds several patents on diabetes drugs, that would be a competitive advantage. It's not just the patents themselves that hold value, the fact that the expectations are that diabetes will continue increasing in the population in the coming years means that the company is well placed for success with its competitive advantages of being able to respond to these changing conditions.

Seek out companies that can weather bad times

Another characteristic that Warren Buffett has long sought is looking for companies that are able to weather downturns in the economy. This can include both major recessions and downturns in the sector where the company is located. Many older companies have shown tremendous resilience, surviving, and even thriving during major economic downturns. A good example is IBM, which has been around for a century, surviving both the Great Depression and the 2008 financial crisis, coming out of both even stronger than it was before. Another characteristic that IBM has is that it has been able to redirect and retool itself for changing market conditions. It is an extremely adaptive company that makes it a good long term investment.

Invest in what you understand

Warren Buffett believes that you should understand the industry a company is in and the products that the industry produces. If you are trying to invest in a sector that you are clueless about, you can't truly evaluate whether a company is a good investment or not. You should be able to look at the products the company is offering, and have a reasonable understanding of their market potential. This means that you need to understand the sector and where it's going. If you know nothing about oil and natural gas, or solar power, then energy companies are probably not a good investment for you. If you are not familiar with real estate, then investing in real estate trusts or exchange-traded funds focused on real estate might not be a good move. Pick a few sectors and learn about the sector as much as you can, so that you can understand the ten year future of the sector and realistically evaluate the sector and the companies in the sector to have an idea of where things are going.

Keep cash available for investing

Warren Buffett advises investors to be prepared for upcoming opportunities. You don't want to sink 100% of your cash into stocks, because new opportunities are always coming up, and you don't want to be in a position where you are not able to take advantage of them. You should be ready to jump into a new stock without having to sell off your existing investments when the investment in a new stock is warranted by the fundamentals of the company and value pricing of the stock. The words "missed opportunity" should not be part of your lexicon. So in order to avoid missed opportunities without having to disrupt your existing portfolio, you should have some cash available at all times to get into new stocks. When you use up the cash, your next goal should be to replenish that supply of cash for when the next opportunity arises.

Have Clear Financial Goals

To follow this type of strategy, you should have clear financial goals in mind. This means that you should know where you want to be in ten, fifteen, and twenty years from now. If you have no idea of where you expect to be in different time frames, then you cannot plan your investing accordingly. Don't have vague goals like "I want to be a millionaire." You should have specific goals that you can use to compare your results to in order to judge the performance of your plan and make the necessary adjustments. If you know that you want to have $100k in stock in five years, then you can figure out how much you need to invest and how often you need to invest. Then when you reach the goal, you can work toward the next goal, which could be $250k in investments.

What the Warren Buffett Investing School Boils Down To

The philosophy that we have described in this chapter comes down to two items. The first is long term investing, and the second is value. So you are looking for value stocks that are priced below market given the value of the company in real terms, and you are looking to hold these investments into your retirement.

Again remember that you are not trying to force yourself into holding investments for the long term, if a company turns out to be a bad choice then you should exit the position and find a better one that is going to help you meet your financial goals.

Chapter 3: Investment Tactics

In this chapter, we are going to discuss the tactics that should be used in conjunction with the *strategy* of Warren Buffett value investing outlined in the previous chapter. Many people misrepresent the methods that we are going to discuss in this chapter as strategies, but in fact, they are tactics, and the strategy is the method you use in order to reach your ultimate financial goals. Tactics are techniques that you employ in your day-to-day operations in order to keep the strategy on track.

There are three main tactics that are used by long term investors in order to further their investment goals and keep their plans on track. These include diversification, dollar-cost averaging, and rebalancing of your portfolio. We will discuss each of these in turn.

Diversification

The most important tactic that you can incorporate into your investing is diversification. The reason is pretty simple and straightforward. First of all, no matter how careful you are in your fundamental analysis, mistakes are going to be made. Also, companies are not always going to stay on the same track going forward. A company might be on solid footing now, but the management may make many mistakes in the coming years, or there could be changes in management or competitors can arise that outcompete the company that you thought was a great investment, causing it to falter.

We have no control over these things. Therefore the best method that can be used to protect yourself is to avoid putting all of your investment money in a single company. In fact, you should avoid putting all of your investment money in a small number of companies. The more companies that you invest in the better off you are, at least in theory.

In practice, you should select a set of companies that you can comfortably manage. The specific number of companies is going to vary from person to person. The more companies that you pick, the more time you are going to have to devote to fundamental analysis and keeping track of stocks and company earnings reports going forward. So there are going to be limits which are different for each person and their living situation. Someone who is a fulltime investor may be able to keep track of a few dozen companies. But someone who has a "day job" and isn't available for more than a few hours a week as far as devoting time to their investments, is not going to be able to keep track of more than a handful of companies.

Therefore we can't say what the exact number of companies to invest in should be. That is going to depend on your situation, but we can say that one company is certainly a bad idea, and 3-4 companies are certainly not enough. Most financial advisors would agree that at a minimum, you should be investing in 7-10 companies. Many financial advisors believe that a good number to shoot for is 20 companies.

If you are not able to invest in more than seven different companies, then perhaps investing in funds is more appropriate. In chapter 9, we will talk about exchange-traded funds. We will discuss the details there, but exchange-tradedfunds allow you to buy shares on the stock market in funds that invest in large numbers of companies. This will help you get the diversified exposure that you need in order to have a healthy portfolio, without having to try and dig up enough companies to do this on your own. You can even invest in funds that are themselves invested in dozens, hundreds, and even thousands of different companies. You can also invest in sectors, different asset classes, and more.

It is important to not only diversify your investments by picking different companies to invest in. They should be in different sectors as well. You don't have to invest in every sector in order to have a diversified portfolio, but you should invest in three different sectors at a minimum. Of course, here we want to be careful, remember one of the dictates of Warren Buffett is that you need to understand what you invest in.

Therefore it's not a good idea to investigate in sectors that leave you feeling clueless. You should pick sectors that you have some general level of understanding in. Or at the very least, if you are considering investing in a sector or industry, take some time to do research and learn all you can about the sector by educating yourself about it. Your education needs to include the past history of the sector as well as an analysis that tells you what companies are poised to dominate the sector in the coming decade. You need to become fully educated in the different products and services offered in the sector, and what analysts think is going to be important going forward.

It's also important not to be investing in sectors that are too closely related, as that would really be the same as investing in one sector. For example, social media and the internet can be considered as distinct, but in reality, social media is a sub-sector of the internet. So while investing in some social media and internet-related companies might be advisable, it is better to invest in 3-4 companies in those areas, while choosing a different and totally unrelated area, like brick and mortar retail (Walmart, Dollar Store, etc.) or pharmaceuticals.

The reason that we seek diversification in our investments is for risk management. This plays out on two levels. The first level where this is influential is in picking out companies to invest in, recognizing that some of the companies are going to fail while others are going to be very successful in the future. At the present day, nobody has a crystal ball that they can use to predict the future. All we can do is use the fundamental analysis in order to play odds. So while we can use probability to our advantage and pick companies that are likely to be successful over the long term, unforeseen events and changes are going to ensure that some of them will fail. The level of failure can happen over a wide range of possibilities. The stock may continue to increase in value, but it may lag that of its competitors. New and different sectors may emerge that make the current sector irrelevant in the future. Consider how unexpected changes can have massive ramifications. We've already talked about fracking, but consider how revolutionary that was. In 2006, oil and gas looked like dinosaurs, and the United States looked as if it would be stuck in a position of having to import the oil and gas it would use. At that time, you would have been making reasonable bets if you were looking into either investing in overseas oil companies or avoiding oil and gas altogether in favor of renewable energy. But then fracking came out of nowhere and completely transformed the energy sector. Rather than having to rely on foreign imports, domestic oil and gas production skyrocketed over the next 10 years, even turning the United States into an exporter of oil and natural gas. Who would have seen that coming?

No matter what sectors you are investing in, you are not going to be able to foresee such changes in most cases. And when they occur, you are not going to be able to know how long they are going to have an impact. Sure, fracking is great for the oil and gas industry now, but where is it going to be in 20 years?

Diversification helps to protect you against these types of risk factors. At a minimum, invest in three different sectors or industries. Then invest in three different companies per sector.

The bottom line is that the more diversified your portfolio is, the better off you are going to be going forward. So you should do the maximum amount of diversification that you can, and if at the present time you are not able to meet a minimum threshold of sectors and companies, then you should consider investing in exchange-traded funds instead so that your exposure is not too limited.

Dollar-Cost Averaging

The next tactic that is used by long term investors is called dollar-cost averaging. The purpose of this method is to avoid getting in a situation where you are buying too much of your stocks when prices are high. As you know, stock prices are constantly fluctuating up and down, and the market itself has many highs and lows including bull and bear markets that take pricing of individual securities along with it for the ride.

Now, over the long term the truth is no matter what you do, the odds are that in ten, twenty, or thirty years, prices are going to be much higher than they are today and so the individual fluctuations are not going to matter that much. But as an investor, you want to maximize your return on investment or ROI. In order for that to happen, so that you can grow your wealth to the maximum extent possible, you need to be buying at the best possible times, when you can get the best possible prices.

Of course, there is one problem with this idea. It comes down to the same basic facts that we discussed in the last section. And that is none of us has a crystal ball despite the claims of some to the contrary. It's simply impossible to know at any given moment whether or not the price of a stock is the best price that is going to be available.

During a bear market, many people are interested in being able to buy stocks when they are "cheap" relative to what they are normally priced. This is a good goal to have, and during bear markets, one of the things that you might consider doing is accelerating your stock purchases.

But one of the problems that happen is people wait too long. They sit on the sidelines hoping to see the stock "hit bottom," but then they find prices suddenly reverse and start rising, and then they end up with a missed opportunity, sometimes even finding that rather than buying cheap stocks they end up paying more for the stock.

Something that every investor needs to get inside their mindset is the fact that nobody knows when a stock or the market at large is going to hit bottom. In truth, you can't possibly know at any given moment if you are paying low or high prices compared to where the stock is going to be in the future. People use technical analysis to try and glean when trends in pricing are going to reverse, but to be honest, that is a lot of gobbledygook. Human behavior is often irrational and impossible to predict, even if "most of the time" you can estimate when there are going to be trend reversals. The methods used in technical analysis are easy to fool by big trading institutions, that can create "signals" by buying or unloading huge quantities of shares simultaneously.

Dollar-cost averaging takes the basic facts into account by recognizing that we are not going to be able to determine with any certainty where tops and bottoms of the market are going to be over the short term. Therefore, it is a method that seeks to buy stocks at averaged out prices. The average over any short term period is going to be low in most cases when compared against the average prices down the road, years and decades into the future. If the average over the short term is not low with respect to future prices, well then you have picked a bad investment.

Another goal that dollar-cost averaging helps you to meet is that it will get you on a regular investment schedule. For long term success in the markets and to build wealth over the long term, you need to invest regularly. Think of this in terms of putting money in the bank. Someone who starts young and puts $100 a month into the bank their entire lives can end up a millionaire by retirement. Dollar-cost averaging can help the stock investor enjoy the same benefits by getting you on a disciplined, and regular investment schedule.

At any given point, you should invest to the maximum extent possible. But to set up a dollar-cost averaging plan, you should figure out a set amount of cash that you are able to invest in the stock market on a regular basis. The amount that you choose should be reasonable so that you have a good probability of meeting your goal at each investment point. The amount that you invest each time can be adjusted with time as you increase your income.

The second part of a dollar-cost averaging plan, which is the most important part of the tactic, is to invest on a regular schedule. You can invest once a week, twice a month, or once a month. As time goes on, you can adjust the schedule as necessary, but the point is that you should have a regular interval that you use in order to make your investments.

By spreading out your investments in this way, you will average out the pricing of the stocks and reduce your risks, while ensuring that you are always investing and sticking to your plans. For example, you might have $500 available each month in order to invest. You can divide this into two investments of $250 each, every two weeks.

When you are able to do it, the best dollar cost averaging plan is going to be the one with more frequent investments. The reason this is the case is that by investing more frequently, you are more accurately averaging out the stock prices. Of course, if your broker charges commissions, you don't want to be investing too much because those expenses can add up over time. But with that in mind, generally speaking investing $50 ten times a month is going to be a better price averaging plan than investing $500 once a month. Of course, the worst thing that you could do would be to invest $6000 once a year.

Before you start investing, look at your monthly budget to figure out a comfortable amount that you can invest each month. This amount should not be large enough that it would interfere with your abilities to pay your monthly living expenses, but it should be the maximum possible amount. Then take that amount and at a minimum, invest it in stocks that you want to include in your plan once a month. If you are able to do it, then invest twice a month or more.

Once you have set upon an amount to invest and an investment schedule, stick to it for the calendar year. Then the first week of each January, re-evaluate your situation and proceed with adjustments if necessary. If you are going to have more income over the coming year, you should definitely adjust the frequency and/or the amounts invested so that you are investing more and possibly more often than you did in the previous year.

Any time that you have extra money to invest, you can do this outside of your regular dollar-cost averaging investment plan. Remember that the rules should be followed but they are not something that has to be written in stone, and adjustments can be made when they are warranted.

Buy More During Downturns

Any time there is a stock downturn, whether it's an individual stock or the market as a whole, you should immediately buy more stock. This is one of the reasons that it's important to have cash on hand. Of course, you don't want to use up all of your cash on a single stock purchase. The reason being that you don't know if the stock is going to keep dropping in price. If it does keep dropping in price, you are going to want to be able to buy more stock at the lower prices. But whenever there is a downward trend in price, you want to put money into the markets so that you can buy the stock at a discount. Of course, we are talking about normal circumstances here. If there is bad news about a company coming out, such as the company is engaged in some kind of fraudulent activity, that is probably not a good reason to be investing more in the company.

What we are talking about here are mundane or external causes. By mundane we mean one bad earnings report among an overall trend of increasing profits. Investors that unload all their Apple stock based on one quarterly report that misses "expectations" or even shows reduced profits are making a foolish play.

External causes can be economic or political in nature. These are news events and such that lead to overall market declines that turn out to be temporary. In fact, these are the reasons that you should use in order to buy more shares.

Rebalancing Your Portfolio

Most investors have their portfolios arranged by class in percentages. They may want to seek out a certain level of aggressive growth, a certain level of value investing, and they also might want to protect a certain amount of their capital. In other words, they use asset allocation to build a portfolio that helps the investor to meet his or her goals over the long term. Asset allocation refers to the way that you have distributed your investments, so for example if we were talking about asset allocation over stocks and bonds, an investor might have 50% of their investments in stocks and 50% in bonds, while a more aggressive investor looking for more growth with higher risk tolerance might have 70% of their investments in stocks and 30% in bonds.

When you first build your investment plans, determining your asset allocation is going to be one of the first things that you do. Someone who needs to raise cash quickly is going to be devoting more of their investments to aggressive growth stocks. Someone who is looking to preserve their money is going to be putting more of it into bonds or money market funds. Everyone has different goals, and you will have to look at your own goals and then breakdown your investment allocations accordingly.

Once you have that setup, you are going to let your investments run for a year and be making your stock purchases at regular intervals in order to meet your goals. So if at the beginning of the year you've decided to invest 65% in stocks, 20% in corporate bonds and 15% in cash, at each point when you make investments you will divide them up this way.

Of course, some investments are going to overperform, and others are going to underperform, with time. So by the end of the year, your portfolio might not be structured in the way you set out to have it structured. You might find that instead, you end up with 70% in stocks, 25% in corporate bonds, and 5% in cash.

At the end of the year, it's time to look at your asset allocation and see if it's remained the same. You will also have to look at your own goals. At the end of the year, your goals might be different than they were at the beginning of the year.

In any case, what you're going to have to do is rebalance your portfolio, either to stay consistent with your original goals or to change the portfolio so that it will help you to meet your new goals. If the percentages in each asset class have changed, and you want to stay consistent with your original goals, you may have to buy and sell assets in order to bring things back into alignment.

Using the previous example, we would have to sell off some stocks and corporate bonds in order to reduce their percentages in the overall portfolio. Then, you would reinvest the proceeds as appropriate to bring yourself back to 65-20-15.

Keep in line using the tactics

The tactics outlined in this chapter are easy to follow, and they are going to help you stay on track to meeting your overall financial goals. The disciplined investor is going to be the one who has the most success over the long term. That means using the Warren Buffett strategies outlined in the previous chapter, in conjunction with using diversification, dollar-cost averaging, and rebalancing your portfolio in order to stay on the road that will lead you toward your financial goals.

Chapter 4: Dividend Stocks

A part of the Warren Buffett investing philosophy is to look for solid companies that pay growing dividends. This can be an important part of your wealth-generating strategy. In the near term, the income from dividend-paying stocks can be used to buy more stocks than you would have been able to purchase otherwise. In other words, rather than taking out the dividends in order to generate income, you would use them to purchase more stock. Of course, by the time that you get close to retirement, you can use the dividend income in order to have cash payments that you can use for income four times a year, as dividends are paid out on a quarterly basis.

The kinds of companies that pay dividends tend to be older and more mature companies. They may be growing companies, but they will be growing at a more modest and sustained rate. These companies may be dominant in their sectors and have a solid market position that is difficult for competitors to challenge. Their share price may be relatively low, compared to upstart challengers or similar companies in the same sector. In other words, in many cases, stocks that are considered to be solid dividend stocks are the kinds of stocks that a Warren Buffett would invest in.

In this chapter, we will learn the basics behind dividend stocks so that you will be educated enough to start investing in these companies and adding them to your portfolio.

What is a Dividend?

Quite simply, a dividend is a cash payment that a corporation makes to the shareholders each quarter. The payments come out of the company's profits. Not all companies pay dividends, those that do are usually more mature companies that have a solid market position, and therefore they are not seeking out aggressive growth. This is not always the case, however. The classic example of dividend companies are older technology companies like IBM and Microsoft, or well-established companies like GE. Other examples include older retail companies like Walgreens or well-established pharmaceutical companies like Abbvie.

Newer, very aggressive companies like Amazon, Facebook, or Netflix are not paying dividends. Rather than share some of their profits with shareholders, these companies are busy reinvesting every last penny that they are able to invest in order to build out their company and expand their market share. However, some companies are in between. The quintessential example of this is Apple, which is a company that has grown very aggressively over the past 20 years, and it's about the same age as Microsoft. However, Apple pays a dividend even though it is considered one of the most aggressive growth companies that are out there in recent years.

Dividends are paid out as cash payment four times a year, at every quarter. However, each company will have its own date when it pays dividends. As an investor, one of the things you will have to familiarize yourself with is knowing when each company you invest in pays out its dividend payments. This is something that you can look up. Knowing the date when this happens can be important as to not only knowing when you get dividend payments but also knowing if you are even eligible to receive the payment for the given quarter.

For any stock, you can look up the ex-dividend date. This is the date by which you must own the shares in order to be eligible for the quarterly dividend payment. The company will have a recording date which is usually two days following the ex-dividend date when they record all stockholders that had shares the day before the ex-dividend date. These are the shareholders that will actually receive dividend payments. So you don't want to be buying your shares on the ex-dividend date.

Dividends are also often paid out for many exchange-traded funds. Whether they are or no is actually up to the manager of the fund. In the case of exchange-traded funds, the dividends that are paid out for all the stocks that pay dividends in the fund directly to the fund. They are then divided up by the shares in the fund, and then if dividends are paid out you will receive payments in proportion to the number of shares that you have in the exchange-traded fund. The dividend payments may be relatively small in some cases, because the fund may not have all stocks paying dividends, but the dividend payments are going to be spread out over the entire investment in the fund.

If a fund manager decides not to pay dividends, the money will be used to buy more shares in the fund on your behalf. So either way, even if the exchange-traded fund does not pay out the cash dividends, if it holds dividend-paying stocks you will benefit by having more shares purchased on your behalf that you will then own.

Dividend Payments and Yield

Two of the important characteristics of a dividend are the yield and the actual payment. Of course, if you are looking to earn a certain amount of money, the amount of the actual dividend payment is going to be something to consider. Payments range over a wide range of values, and they are quoted in annual amounts. So to get the amount that you will receive each quarter simply divide the reported amount by 4.

Many dividends pay in the annual range of $1.50 per share up to $20 per share. As an example, IBM pays around $6 per share annually, while Apple pays around $1.59-$2 per share. While the amount of the dividend payment can help you determine how many shares you need in order to get a certain level of income from the dividend payments, you also need to consider the yield. This is the ratio of the dividend payment to the share price. That gives you an idea of how much you have to invest, rather than just knowing how many shares that you need. If there is a higher yield, this can indicate that the share price of the stock is relatively low in comparison to a stock with a low yield.

There are a couple of things to look for when considering dividend-paying stocks beyond the fundamentals discussed in the second chapter. First of all, you want to be able to review how the dividend payments have changed with time. A stock that shows a long term history of increasing dividend payments is going to be a preferred investment. At the very least, the dividend payments should be keeping up with inflation. You can look up the history of dividend payments for any company.

If the company tends to be one that slashes dividends at the slightest excuse, that may be one that you want to stay away from. You are going to be more interested in dividend stocks that try and keep investors happy even when the stock or the economy at large may be going through some temporary difficulties. In recent times, you can check to see how stocks dealt with the great recession in order to find the best dividend-paying stocks when it comes to the company dealing with hard times.

In addition to the history of dividend payments, you will want to look at a couple of things. One is the dividend payout ratio. The dividend payout ratio is the fraction of its net income that it pays out to investors. Generally speaking, any value of 60% or lower is considered healthy. This indicates that the company has a lot of profits leftover that it could use to increase dividend payments. In addition, it shows that the company is making dividend payments comfortably. That also tells you that the company has some profits leftover that it can reinvest in order to keep the company growing and for research and development, and that it's less likely to need to take on debt in order to keep operating.

On the other hand, if the number is approaching 100%, that is something you need to watch out for. This may be a red flag that the company has some bad fundamentals, and so it is trying to make up for that and keep investment in the stock appealing by paying high dividends. Some companies will even be paying over 100%. In that case, an investigation is necessary. Are they paying more than 100% in a temporary fashion? If it's just a phenomenon occurring over a couple of quarters, then it might not be a catastrophic warning sign. But something to consider, especially if this is a continual practice, is that the company is having trouble or taking on too much debt. The company may even be using debt to keep dividend payments higher than they would be otherwise. This is not only bad news as to the future health of the company and possibly for its stock price but also an indicator that they may not be able to keep up their dividend payments over the long term.

The amount of debt that a company is taking on can also be an important factor when investigating dividend-paying stocks. A company that takes on a lot of debt can be problematic for many reasons. Of course, more debt can mean less health, but at the same time, a company can be healthy and temporarily take on some debt. On the other hand, something that needs to be considered is that when a company takes on debt, they are required to make interest payments on the debt, and when the debt matures they have to pay back the principal. Those may be obvious facts, but what may not be so obvious is the fact that a company that has to make ever-increasing interest payments is also one that might have trouble finding money left over in order to make consistent dividend payments.

As an investor in dividend-paying stocks, the last thing that you are going to want is a stock that you cannot rely on for income. So all of these factors need to be considered when looking for a good stock to invest in.

Using Dividend Paying Investments for Diversification

One of the most interesting things about dividend-paying stocks is that there are many which are specific for different sectors, that will help you diversify your overall portfolio. One of the most popular ways that people invest in order to get dividend payments on the stock market is to invest in real estate investment trusts, which go by the shorthand name of REIT. These companies trade on the stock exchanges and you buy shares of stock in them and receive dividend payments just like you would for a corporation, however, these are not corporations. They are a special class of business organization that is called a trust, and they payout 90% of their profits to investors. They often have relatively low share prices and high yields, making them an attractive investment if you are looking for high yield dividend payments. Moreover, they are invested in a wide range of real estate projects, from cell phone towers to old age facilities while also investing in conventional real estate projects like single-family homes, apartments, commercial office space, and retail space. Investors can also sign up with fundrise, which enables them to invest in real estate and receive dividend payments. These are generally considered reliable investments because they get their money through the rental income stream that goes to the properties themselves.

There are other options that you can also invest in using the stock market. MLPs are a type of partnership that is actually traded on the stock exchange, that lets you invest in finance and energy companies. Most MLPs are involved in the oil and natural gas business. There are also BDCs, which are business development companies. These types of organizations invest in distressed companies or offer to finance through unconventional means for companies that might have credit problems and therefore not be able to get traditional bank loans. These types of companies tend to have high dividend yields, and most have low share prices.

DRIPS

A DRIP is a dividend reinvestment plan. The nature of this plan is to automatically use your dividends to buy more shares of stock. You can elect to have this setup with your broker. The time to use DRIPS is when you are in the growth phase of your investment career, and so you are waiting until later in order to cash out your stocks to get income from them. In the case of dividend stocks, of course, you are not going to be selling off your shares. You are going to be interested in holding your shares in order to receive the cash income from your dividend payments. Typically this is going to be something that you are interested in doing in retirement. Before then, you are going to want to continue growing the number of shares that you own so that you can maximize your income later.

DRIPS provide a way to add more power to this by purchasing more shares as you go along. So if you are investing in a $30 stock that you earn $120 in the given quarter from in the form of dividend payments, you can reinvest that $120 back into your stock to buy four more shares of it each quarter. Over the years, the extra shares that you acquire by investing using DRIPS can really add up, helping you to grow your wealth even more over time. This is the smarter way to invest even though the temptation at times is going to be to take out the money and spend it. The best thing to do is to have your broker set this up to work automatically until you tell them otherwise so that the temptation on your end is removed as a factor.

Then when you reach the point where you are ready to retire, you can change your election as far as DRIPs are concerned and start receiving the cash payments for the income that you seek.

Dividend Stocks – The Bottom Line

Dividend stocks are something to consider investing in as a part of your overall investment plan. However, it's important to be realistic about dividend-paying stocks. Most of them pay relatively small payments on a per-share basis. What this means as far as a practical matter is that you are going to need to acquire a large number of shares in order to get significant dividend income from them. For example, if a stock pays $6 dividend payments, you need 7,000 shares in order to earn $42,000 a year. If the stock is trading at $100 a share, that means you would need to invest $700,000 in order to get that income. Of course, there are stocks and other types of investments such as REITs that pay a wide range of yields, and so the amounts required vary. Also, people should be thinking in terms of long term investing, but it's clear that to make money from dividends you are going to be needing to develop a serious investment program as a part of your overall strategy.

Chapter 5: Becoming a Stock Trader

Most people have their investments, if they have investments at all, managed by someone else. In most cases, this is going to be in a 401 (k) through their employer. Many people who take the next steps in investing outside of that will do it passively, handing over a large amount of cash for investment in a mutual fund or an individual retirement account or IRA.

With that in mind, taking direct control over your investing and becoming an individual, self-directed investor is quite a different approach for many people. They are not sure how to do it or even where to start. The issues that we have discussed so far are definitely going to be important, but you have to know how to actually buy and sell stocks in order to get going with your plans. The first step in this direction is opening a brokerage account.

In this chapter, we are going to introduce you to the basic setup of opening your account and how to trade stocks. The process is really not that complicated, but it can be daunting for the new investor.

What is a brokerage?

As an individual investor, you are not going to run down to the trading floor of a stock exchange and place your own orders. Investors use a middle man that accomplishes this for them. That middle man is called a stock brokerage, or simply a brokerage or broker. There are many companies that fill this role today, and it's pretty easy to find them. Just google "Brokerage," and you can find many websites that will do this for you.

For people new to the life of trading stocks as an individual, this can be an intimidating process because you may not really know who is legitimate and who isn't. We can start with some of the big names in finance, that you may recognize. We hope that in this book, we are able to give readers enough information that they can comfortably open a trading account with some level of confidence. Of course, you are going to want to be sure that the money you invest in your account is safe and secure, and that you are not being taken by a shady broker that can charge high commissions.

The first rule of thumb is to stick to brokers that are licensed and located in your own country. In the United States, brokers are strictly regulated by the U.S. Securities and Exchange Commission, or SEC.

As we said, there are many famous financial names, but not everyone may be aware of them. Let's start with the top four. These include Fidelity Investments, Charles Schwab, Ally Bank, and Merryl (formerly Merryl Lynch, a very old company). These are not "the top 4" in terms of quality or recommendation, but we have listed four companies that have been well known in the investment world for decades, and therefore these are definitely companies that you can trust as far as having an account that is safe and so forth.

However, there are many others. Two companies that gained a lot of fame as brokers during the go-go stock days of the dot com era in the late 1990s are TD Ameritrade and E*Trade. Actually, both companies were formed long before the dot com boom, TD Ameritrade began operation in the early 1970s, and E*Trade opened its doors about ten years later.

There are many newer platforms, some of which are operated by older companies and some that are independent. You can invest in using websites called think or swim, and tasty works. These forums are more geared toward speculators and options traders, however.

There are also some newer platforms that operate in the mobile app space. Robinhood is the most famous example. It's become very popular with new investors because it's extremely easy to use and it also comes with zero commission trading.

If you choose any of the brokers above, you won't have any problems. Some are preferred by some financial experts over others, but all are reliable and fairly easy to use. You can also access all of them via a desktop computer or mobile app, which means they are user-friendly and readily accessible.

Commissions

One of the issues with brokers is commissions. As a long term investor, this is less of a concern than it would be if you were trading at a high-frequency level. The industry range of commissions tends to be over $5-$7 per trade. So it's not a huge expense unless you are making several trades a week. That said, keeping expenses to a minimum is something that a lot of investors like to do and with good reason. There are many companies that offer zero commission trading, Robinhood being one of the more recent entries into this space. If you can completely eliminate commissions, that is certainly helpful for your overall bottom line.

Some, like Charles Schwab, offer no commission trading on certain exchange-tradedfunds. This can be helpful if you happen to be investing in the funds that they allow this for, but for your other trades, you will still have to pay commissions. Some may offer reduced commissions under certain circumstances.

Generally speaking, while its certainly attractive to be in a situation where you can trade without paying any commissions at all, most long term investors are not going to be too concerned with the commissions paid because they are not going to be trading all that frequently. Also, the dollar magnitude of the commissions is not all that high in most cases. Something that has to be weighed is the amount paid for the commission against the longevity of the broker. That is many brokers like Charles Schwab have been in business for some time, while others like Robinhood that charge zero commissions are relatively new. The thing to do is get online and research the different brokers to see which one appeals to you the most.

In order to set up a brokerage account, you will have to enter basic information about yourself, such as name and address. You will also have to electronically connect a bank account that can be used to fund the brokerage account. Some brokerages have a minimum funding requirement while others will let you fund it with whatever amount you choose.

Margin Accounts

A margin account lets you borrow money and stock from the broker. You have to put up 50% of your own cash to fund any trade. The amount of cash that you put up for a trade is called the margin. So for the stock market, you have 2:1 leverage, which means that you have twice the purchasing power of the actual dollar amount used to fund the margin account. To open a margin account, you must deposit $2,000. A margin account should not be used for long term investing, because you have to pay interest on any borrowed funds. The primary use of a margin account would be for trading so that you could return the funds borrowed in a prompt fashion.

How to Trade Stocks

Once you have funded your account, you can start buying shares. The details of how to do it vary, because they are specific to the brokerage selected. But essentially this will involve looking up the stock that you are interested in buying or selling, and then after that, it will be like buying something on Amazon or any other website. You just specify how many shares you want to buy, and if you have the adequate amount of funding in your brokerage account, you can just buy the shares. Some brokerages will allow you to instantly fund your account, but with others, you may have to wait until the bank actually deposits the money.

Money Management and Risks

It's important that you do proper money management when buying stocks, especially if you are looking to trade. One rule that always applies is that you should never invest more money than you can afford to lose. So, each month limit yourself to putting in a specific amount into your account that should you lose the money, it will have no impact on your day to day life. Of course, losing money always has an impact, but what we mean here is that if you lost the money, you will still be able to pay your rent or mortgage, buy your groceries, and so forth.

We have talked about the risk management techniques for long term investing; these involve diversification, dollar-cost averaging, and rebalancing your portfolio. If you are interested in trading, then you are going to focus your risk management efforts on ensuring that you are not going to lose more than a certain portion of your account value on any given trade.

Chapter 6: How the Stock Market Works

In this chapter, we will briefly review the concept of the stock market and the roles of different players. We will formalize the concept of stocks and how stocks are valued in the marketplace.

What are stocks?

Stock is a term which refers to the capital that a company raises by issuing shares. When you buy shares, you are giving the capital (the "stock") to the company that it can use to fund its operations. So the company can use the money raised by issuing shares of stock to hire employees, fund marketing and advertising efforts, build new manufacturing plants, or any other activity that the company needs funds to carry out.

The "stock" of the company is divided up into individual shares. So a company could start out with a "stock" of a million dollars, and divide that up into 10,000 "shares of stock" that it could then sell to the public for $100 a share. When you buy a share, you own a "share" of the company.

Of course, to own 25% of a company worth $1 million, you would have to buy $250,000 worth of shares, or 2,500 shares.

Like anything else, once you've bought something you have a right to sell it. The cumbersome way to deal with this would be to sell it back to the company, who could then find another buyer. However, as soon as the concept of stock in a company was devised, people developed markets for secondary trading of shares of stock. So rather than going through the company, and having the company deal with the problem of finding new investors, people could trade stocks back and forth amongst themselves. This was the birth of the first stock markets.

This created a situation where the value of the shares, and therefore of the company itself, would change with time. As the company became seen as more valuable, perhaps because it was making more profits, people would bid up the prices of shares sold in the stock markets. More people would be interested in buying an ownership stake in a successful business, and many of them would be willing to pay more money in order to own shares of the stock.

At the same time, companies that were not doing well would become less valuable. If a company was losing money or simply not operating at a very profitable level, fewer people would be interested in owning stock in the company. Those that did who wanted to get out of their ownership stake would lower the prices they are willing to accept in order to get rid of their stock. As a result, the price of the shares of a company having problems will drop in value.

The role of brokers

In modern stock markets, you don't get in your car and drive down to some market in order to sell your shares of stock, which we might imagine that you are carrying around as certificates in an envelope. First of all, today's markets are all electronic. But we do have trading floors. Your orders to buy and sell stocks happen on the trading floor, but you are not directly placing them.

You are placing your orders to buy and sell shares of stock through a middleman that is the broker you are using. So you pay them a fee, and they actually carry out the trade for you, as we mentioned earlier. The trades are not automatic although they often seem that way today with the fast-paced electronic transactions. You actually have to find a buyer when you sell a share of stock. The buyer has to agree to the price you are asking for the transaction to occur. When you enter into a trade, there is no telling who you are trading with. It could be another individual trader like you, a hedge fund, or an institutional trader such as a large pension fund.

Types of Orders

When trading stock, there are several types of orders that can be placed. The basic order type is a market order, and this is the default type of order that is placed. If you don't specify any order type, your broker is going to place a market order. These are the specific order types that can be used:

- Market Order: This is an order that will buy or sell shares of stock at the prevailing market price. Most of the time market orders are carried out very quickly, in the blink of an eye in today's electronic trading world. However, if a stock is rapidly dropping in value or rising in value, a market order might not be carried out. Under most circumstances, this is not going to happen.

- Limit Order: This is an order to only carry out the buying or selling order at a price that you specify. For example, if a stock is trading at $50 a share, you might enter a limit order if you are only willing to buy it at $49 a share. So you can specify this as your limit price, and the order will only be carried out if the stock price drops to $49 and you find someone willing to trade at that price. There are two types of limit orders. The default type of limit order is good until the end of the day order. So if it is not carried out by the end of the day, the order will be canceled. You can also set up good until canceled limit order. The order will remain in place until it's either fulfilled or you manually cancel it.

- Stop Loss: A stop-loss order is an order to automatically sell shares of stock that you buy if the share price drops to a value that you specify. Stop-loss orders are used by day or swing traders in order to get out of bad trades. It will not be executed if the share price of the stock does not drop to the value specified. However, if the share price does drop at or below the value specified, it will be carried out automatically and your shares will be sold.

- Stop Limit: Also known as a take profit order. This is analogous to a stop-loss order. However, this is an order to sell the stock if the price rises to a value that you specify. The order will only be carried out if the price rises to the given value.

Bid/Ask

Pricing of stocks is determined by supply and demand.

At any given time, you can see what values traders are using to bid for prices. Bid, is the value being offered by traders looking to buy a stock. That is it's the highest price they are willing to pay in order to buy the stock. If the stock price is dropping and for some reason, your sell order doesn't go through, that may be because the bid price has dropped well below the price you are asking for in your market or limit order. Ask is the price that people who are trying to sell the stock are asking for it. These are average values, of course. When there is a large bid-ask spread it can be hard to sell the stock unless you are willing to adjust your price down to the bid value and sell it in a limit order. The market price is not going to match up with the bid price in many cases, but if the bid-ask spread is narrow and the stock is one that has a high trading volume, it is easy to find a buyer.

Your broker will provide you with the tools needed to find the bid and ask as well as the market price for any stock that is being traded.

Volume

Volume is the number of times or number of times that the stock was traded in the last trading period. Depending on the time scales you are using on your stock charts, the volume could be the number of times the stock was traded per minute, per hour, or per day. In most cases, when the volume is reported, the volume of trading for the previous trading day is given.

P/E Ratio

The price to earnings ratio, or P/E ratio, is a metric that is commonly used in order to estimate the value of a given stock. There is not an absolute standard that is used for the P/E ratio. What you have to do with the P/E ratio, is look at the value of the stock and then compare it to different metrics. The most important comparison to make is to see how the P/E ratio compares to the values of its nearest competitors and the sector itself that it is trading in. If it's a large company, you can also compare it to the average P/E ratio for the S & P 500 index. For different sized companies, you can compare to other relevant indexes. If this value is high relative to other companies in the same sector and that is about the same size, that can mean that the stock is overpriced. But it can also simply mean that the stock is highly prized. The company might have a disruptive product it is releasing, for example.

Company Size

Something you will be interested in when it comes to investing in the company size. Traders are not interested in company size, so much as they are only interested in how much the stock might be moving on a given day. However, long term investors need to keep track of company size because the size of a company is something that can be associated with many things. First of all, for publicly traded companies, the smaller size means that the company probably has a lot of room to grow. So smaller and mid-sized companies are considered to have growth potential, and those looking to have aggressive growth in the value of their stock portfolio are going to want to put more of their investment capital in these types of companies. However, the smaller companies are not as stable as large companies that are hard to knock off their pedestal like Apple or Boeing. They are often new, and they are also often more likely to fail as time goes on. This is the trade-off that is made here, smaller companies have a lot of growth potential, but they also carry a much higher risk of failure – and so the investor will have some risk of losing some or even all of their investment capital. The problem is ahead of time you can't know which companies that are small now are going to be the giants 20 years down the road. Companies are classified according to size or market capitalization, which is the amount of money invested in the company.

Companies are generally divided by market size in the following way:

- Nano-Cap: $50 Million or less. High risk, but could have large potential gains. These are usually "penny stocks," which means the share price is $5 or less. They are risky investments but popular with traders because they can have large price movements over short time periods.
- Micro-Cap: $50 million to $300 million. Still high risk but more stable than nano-cap stocks.

- Small-Cap: $300 million to $2 billion. Getting better, larger companies that are more likely to weather storms, lots of growth potential, but still relatively risky.

- Mid-Cap: $1 billion up to $5 billion in valuation. These are good stocks that kind of balance the risk with potential rewards. Companies this big are not nearly as risky as the others considered so far, but they do have more risk than large-cap firms, generally speaking. The trade-off is more growth potential, provided that you are able to pick the right firms to invest in.

- Large-Cap: $5 billion or more. Large companies that are lower risk, but also offer lower average growth potential.

- Mega-Cap: The biggest of the big, with $200 billion or more in market capitalization.

How to Mitigate Risk While Still Going for Growth

The way to mitigate risk among mid-cap and small-cap companies while taking advantage of the growth potential is diversification. Most of us are probably not going to be able to determine which mid-cap or small-cap companies are going to be growing by significant amounts over the coming years, but if you have a diversified portfolio of these kinds of companies you significantly increase your odds of getting some winners. The best way to do this is by using exchange-traded funds that might invest in hundreds or more of these companies. That way your risk is spread out, and the fund itself will be picking the best companies to invest in, and that can give you exposure to these companies with lower overall risk. Then you can take advantage of the aggressive growth that the winners among the small and mid-cap firms have to offer.

Also, keep in mind that many large-cap and even mega-cap firms are also still experiencing strong growth. High-tech companies are an example of this.

How to Invest in the Stock Market

Many people are invested in the stock market through their employers, using a 401k plan. These plans may invest in individual stocks, or they may buy into mutual funds, which are pooled funds of money that buy large amounts of shares in a diverse array of stocks. Another way that people invest in the stock market is by investing in mutual funds on their own, through a mutual fund company. There are small mutual fund companies that you can probably find in your own town, or you might invest in large mutual fund companies online such as Vanguard or Fidelity.

Individual investors can also use an individual retirement account or IRA to invest in the stock market. IRA's are limited because of the tax benefits. You can invest $6,000 a year before age 50, and if you are 50 or older, you can invest $7,000 a year into an IRA. An IRA has tax benefits. For a Roth IRA, which has income limits, you will be able to withdraw the money from the IRA in retirement tax-free. If the IRA is a traditional IRA, you can deduct your investments into the IRA on your current taxes, but you will have to pay taxes on the money that you take out of the IRA in retirement.

Using a brokerage, you can also buy and sell stocks on your own. This is the way to proceed if you want to have a self-directed investment plan. Of course, it's possible to have a multi-leg investment plan. That is, you could use an IRA, and also do self-directed stock investing outside the IRA.

As we will see there is also the possibility of investing in the stock market as an individual investor while buying shares of exchange-traded funds. While there are some differences, this is similar to investing in mutual funds, but this is something that you would do as a self-directed investor.

Chapter 7: Swing Trading

We have already spent a great deal of time talking about long term investing with stocks. This is my preferred method of working with the stock market. You invest in companies for the long term with the goal of building long term wealth. However, there are certainly ways that you can trade stocks in order to earn short term cash. The main ways that this is done include day trading and swing trading. Day trading is a highly specialized field that involves a lot of money and risk. In order to be a day trader, you must deposit $25,000 in a margin account. Day trading is a regulated activity, and your broker will differentiate between day traders and others that are not considered as day traders because day trading is a high-risk activity.

However, there is another method of trading which is considered not as risky, called swing trading. The method behind swing trading is to focus on the swings that occur in the stock market on a regular basis in order to earn profits. So it's basically a buy low and sell high philosophy, but the swing trader holds their positions from days to weeks, and so is not at as high of a risk as a day trader. For this reason, it is not a regulated field. In this chapter, we are going to talk about swing trading as an alternative method.

Why Swing Trade?

Swing trading is an entirely different style and method as compared to long term investing and the methods used by Warren Buffett. In fact, Warren Buffett would not approve of swing trading at all, and he would consider it to be a form of gambling.

His attitude may be a bit harsh, however. Day trading, which is a form of trading that requires full-time attention to the markets and you cannot hold your positions overnight without carrying serious risk, might be more akin to gambling. However, with swing trading, we wait for the inevitable ups and downs that always occur in the markets.

But what is the purpose of swing trading? While the goal of long term investing is to build wealth over time, swing trading is not investing. It is a business that is focused on earning cash profits in the present.

As a swing trader, you are not really interested in the underlying stock, other than asking the question – is the price of the stock going to move by a significant amount in the near future.

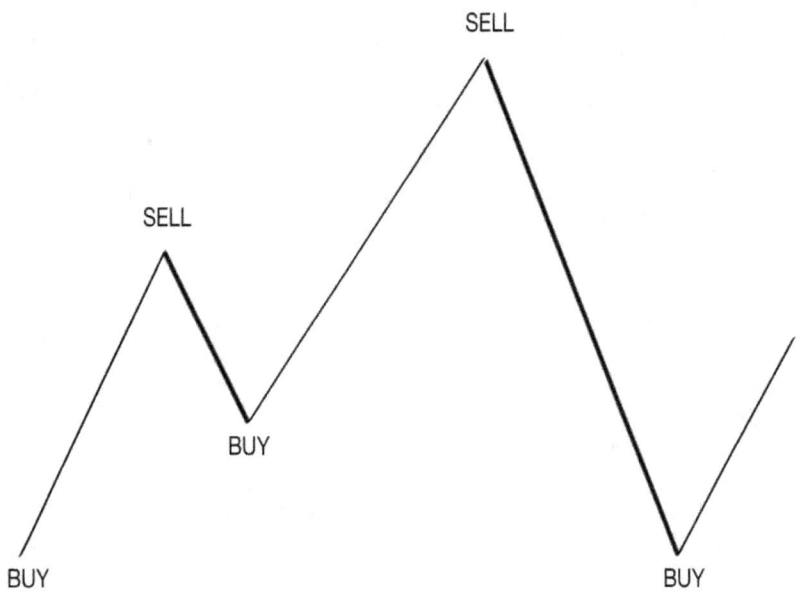

As seen in the figure above, the price of a stock is going to go up and down in repeated fashion, depending on the time period involved. The idea behind swing trading is simple – you buy low and sell high. So you can be said to be trading with the swings.

So if a stock is trading at a relative low of $50 a share, a swing trader may buy a large number of shares in anticipation of it rising to a recent high of $55 a share, then they can sell at that point and take the profit of $5 a share. A swing trader can trade using a margin account, but if you are able to and willing to put up your own cash to cover the trades, you don't have to use a margin account in order to engage in swing trading.

Types of Stocks to trade while swing trading

You can trade any type of stock while swing trading. The key to swing trading is to look for stocks that are having or expected to have large price swings in the market over the near term. Different swing traders have different time frames, but all swing traders are going to hold their positions at least overnight. Some are looking to make gains over the short term, so maybe over a couple of days or a few days. Other swing traders are willing to wait several weeks in order to sell their shares, or even over the course of a couple of months.

There is not a set time for swing trading, in the way that there is for day trading. When you are swing trading, you will hold onto your positions until the time is right to sell. Of course, this is not always going to work out, and you might have to exit your position and take a loss. There is always risk involved in swing trading.

So rather than looking to trade specific stocks, a swing trader is trying to find stocks that are volatile and having a lot of price movements. If a stock crashes down to a relatively low price, the swing trader will see this as an opportunity to buy stock at a discount, so that he or she can sell it later on when the price rebounds to a higher level.

Trending stocks are the ideal type of trade for the swing trader. Sometimes stocks will go into a long term trend where the price may move up and down by small amounts over short time periods, but over the course of a week or months, the stock is on a long term upward trend.

The chart below illustrates the concept of a long term, upward trend.

Shorting Stock

It's also possible for a trader to make money shorting the stock. This means you are betting that the price of the stock is going to drop. As you can imagine, stocks don't just go into upward trends. They also go into long term downtrends if there is bad news about the company. If there is a bad earnings call, a stock can suffer through a catastrophic decline for a day or two, or even up to a week. These kinds of price drops offer opportunities for people to profit by shorting stock. In order to short stock, you need to have a margin account. Then you borrow shares of the stock that you think is going to drop from the broker. Then you sell them on the open market. Let's say that you can borrow shares of a stock that is trading at $100 a share, so you borrow 500 shares and sell them for $50,000. Now suppose that the company has a bad earnings call. Then the share price drops to $35 a share. So you can buy them back at this reduced price for $35,000. This means that you've made a profit of $15,000. Now you also have the shares back in your possession, which you can then return to the broker.

Chart Patterns

In order to be a successful swing trader, you need to understand stock market charts and technical indicators. A part of this is recognizing chart patterns that generally indicate that a current trend is about to reverse. In other words, if the stock has been declining in price, certain chart patterns will indicate that the stock is about increasing in price. Conversely, there are chart patterns that can indicate when a stock that has been on an upward price trend is about to reverse course and begin a downward trend in price.

If you are buying stock in the hopes that the price is going to rise, you are said to be "long" on the stock. In this case, you are looking for the reversal of a downward trend in order to find the best possible price to buy the stocks. Then you will wait until the price rises to a point where it begins showing signs that it is going to decline again. At this point, you will sell your shares.

If you are looking to short the market, you are going to use the same signals to buy and sell shares. However, you're going to enter your position at the peak, while the trader with the long position is exiting their position at the peak price. So when you see that the signals are there for a trend reversal after there has been an upward trend in price, you will borrow the shares from the broker and immediately sell them. Then you will wait until the stock price declines in value and starts showing signs of another trend reversal. We can have reasonable assurance that the stock has reached a low price before it is going to go up in price again. Then we can go ahead and buy the shares back, and return them to the broker.

What you are going to look for are signals that the price trend is "trying" to continue, but there simply isn't enough momentum. Let's start by considering an upward trend in price. When the price has peaked, the stock may be overvalued, and although some buyers are going to continue entering the market, they are not going to be able to bid up the price of the stock very much, or for very long. So you will see small price peaks, perhaps repeated, but the price just won't go any higher. This indicates a shifting momentum, and it's only a matter of time before the price will drop back down.

The patterns that you will see are called head and shoulders, cup and handles, double top, and the rising wedge. The shape of these patterns is shown below.

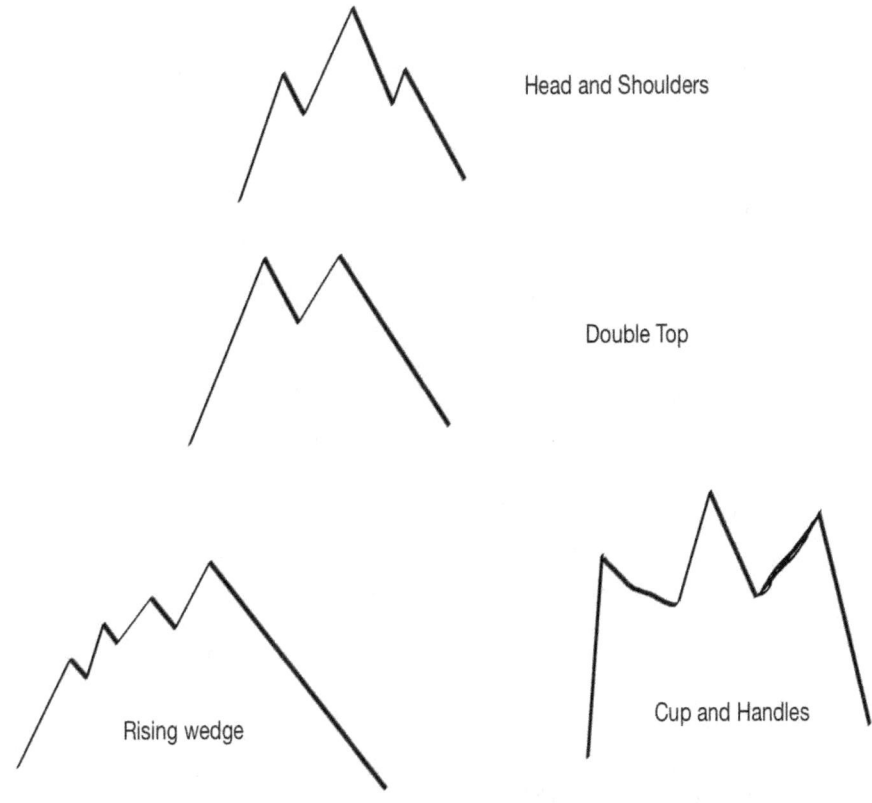

Head and Shoulders

Double Top

Rising wedge

Cup and Handles

The same patterns will occur at the end of a downtrend, but they are going to be flipped over. So in a downtrend, a point will be reached when bearish investors are still trying to get rid of their stocks, but the trend has lost momentum and people are starting to bid up prices again. An example of this is shown below, with the inverted double top.

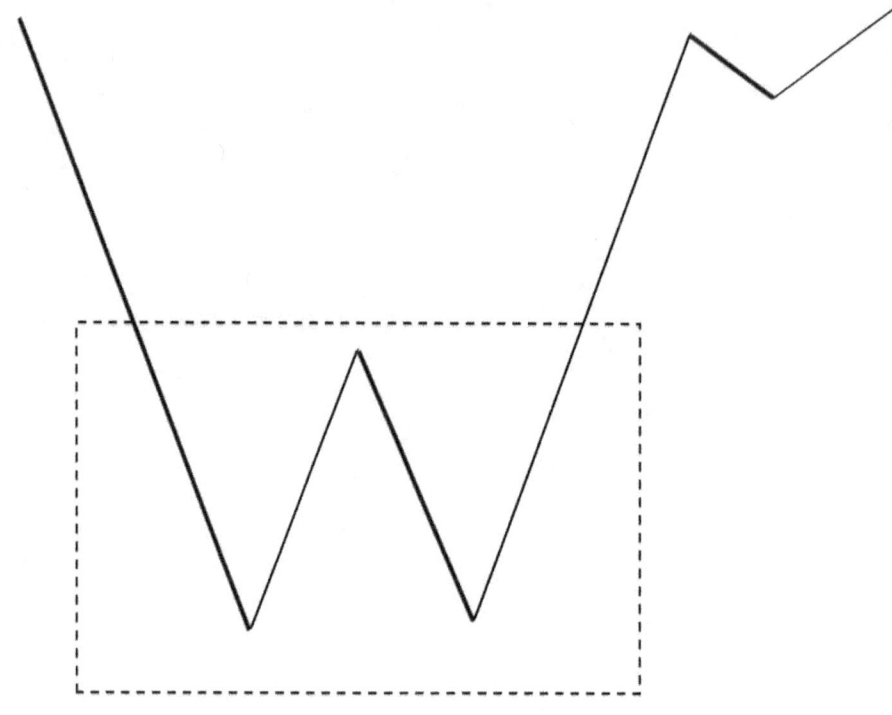

Candlestick Charts

Most traders will use candlestick charts in order to get more detailed information about the behavior of traders and price movements. Candlesticks are red or green bars on stock charts. The bars have small lines that may stick out one or both ends that are called shadows or various wicks. The wicks indicate the high and low prices for each bar, where a bar represents a trading period of a length that you can define on the chart. Day traders might be looking at one minute and five-minute trading sessions. Swing traders may look at short term trading sessions when looking to enter and exit a trade but generally swing traders are interested in longer-term price shifts and so will be looking at daily candles in most cases.

The color of the candle indicates whether the price rose during the trading session, in which case the candle is colored green, or whether the price fell during the trading session, in which case the candle is colored red. These are known as bullish and bearish candlesticks.

For a green or bullish candlestick, the bottom of the body or the bar is the opening price for the trading session. The top of the body is then the closing price for the trading session. This reflects the fact that for the trading session, the price closed higher than it opened at. For a bearish candlestick, the price closes at a lower price than it opened for the session. That means that the top of the bearish candlestick is the opening price for the trading session, while the bottom of the candlestick is the opening price for the trading session.

Traders learn different patterns that occur in candlestick charts that tend to indicate coming price reversals. For example, at the bottom of a downtrend, before a price reversal, you will often see a bearish candlestick followed by a much larger green or bullish candlestick, a trading session during which the closing price was pushed much higher. Or you may see the corresponding pattern in reverse at the top of an uptrend. That is, a bullish candlestick will be followed by a much larger bearish candlestick, that indicates the priced was pushed low during that trading session. This reversal pattern is called the engulfing candlestick.

Another common pattern that you look for indicating a reversal is three candlesticks of the same color, each with succeeding higher closing prices at the close of each trading session. This is called three white soldiers. Alternatively, you can be at the top of an uptrend, and then see three bearish candlesticks in a row with three successive lower closing prices. That indicates the trend is reversing.

An indecision candlestick is one that has a flat body, with no width. That is, the opening and closing prices are going to be the same or close to being the same for the trading session. The candlestick may have long wicks, which indicates the price was pushed high and low during the trading session but then ended up where it started. Sometimes there are no wicks at all. In either case, these are called indecision candlesticks. They also go by their Japanese name, which is doji candlesticks.

Another candlestick that is considered important is a hammer. This is a candlestick with a small body and a long wick sticking out of the bottom. This indicates that the price opened at a certain level, but was pushed down to a very low price during the trading session. But then it rebounded and closed higher. So this would be a green or bullish candlestick. You would look for it at the bottom of a downtrend, and it is taken as a strong signal of a coming uptrend.

If the candlestick is flipped over, you get a "shooting star." So you will have a short body with a long wick sticking out of the top. In this case, we are looking for a bearish candlestick which will be red in color, occurring in the midst of an uptrend. This is taken as a signal of a coming downtrend since the price was pushed up high but ended up closing low.

There are many other candlestick patterns that you can study which are related to shifts or trend reversals. You can find them in any book on the day or swing trading, and there are many online resources that are available that can teach you all of the candlestick patterns that you need to learn how to recognize as a swing trader.

Technical Indicators

Technical indicators are purported to indicate future trends in pricing. The main ones that swing traders use are moving averages and the relative strength indicator, along with a more sophisticated tool that is called Bollinger bands. Let's take a brief look at each of these. If you are more interested in pursuing swing trading, you should get a book specifically devoted to the topic where you can learn the details behind these tools.

Moving averages are pretty simple to understand. You simply take the closing prices of the past x number of trading sessions and average them together at each point. A moving average removes the noise from a stock market chart and produces a smooth curve. There are several ways that moving averages can be calculated, but the most common types of moving averages that are used by swing traders include simple moving averages and exponential moving averages. The differences between the two are that an exponential moving average gives a larger weight to more recent prices.

The key to moving averages is that you can plot moving averages for different numbers of trading sessions. So, you can have a short period or a long period moving average, using a small number or a larger number of trading sessions to calculate the moving average. The trader will plot both on the same stock chart. Then they look at the movements of the short term moving average with respect to the long term moving average. If the short term moving average crosses above the long term moving average, that means that the trend is going to be an upward trend in price. On the other hand, if the moving average moves below the long term moving average, that would indicate a coming downturn in price.

Traders prefer not to work in isolation, in the sense that you don't want to be stuck using only one clue in order to make your trades. What they want to see is multiple signals that all agree, so you would want to see candlestick patterns indicating changes in the trend that are confirmed with moving averages.

The relative strength indicator or RSI is very popular. This is a graph that you can add below your stock chart. The main thing that the RSI indicates is whether or not a stock is overbought or underbought. The RSI can range from 0 to 100. If the RSI goes above 80, these are overbought conditions. That is, the price has been big up too high with respect to the actual demand that exists in the market. This can indicate it's a good time to sell shares. The best thing to do, however, is to use this in conjunction with other signals, in particular with the moving averages.

If the RSI drops below 20, the opposite condition is reached, that is the RSI is telling you that the stock is oversold. That means that the stock is likely to see a trend reversal and prices are likely to climb. Again, you will want to use the RSI in conjunction with other signals, and not use it in isolation.

Finally, we will take a look at Bollinger bands. The Bollinger band is made up of three curves. In the middle, you will find a 20 period moving average. Then there are upper and lower curves, which indicate one standard deviation above the average price and one standard deviation below the moving average. Traders expect a reversal when the price meets or exceeds the one standard deviation curve.

Support and Resistance

Sometimes, in fact, most of the time, a stock is not in a big trend. Instead, the stock is probably moving up and down in a relatively small range of prices. This is called ranging. There are opportunities for swing traders to make profits with ranging stocks since the price is bouncing up and down between two known price levels for an extended period of time.

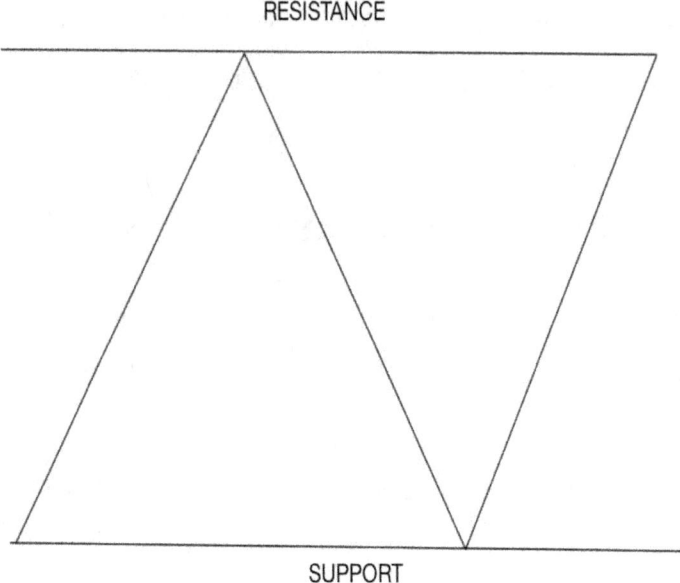

RESISTANCE

SUPPORT

The bottom price that the stock reaches is called support. The term support means that the stock is unlikely to break lower to the downside. You need to see the stock price touch the support level at least twice. The support level is a price at which you should buy shares.

If the stock is truly ranging, it will then rise up to a high price level where it's not likely or able to break above. Again, you will want to see it touch that price level two or more times. The resistance price level is the price at which you would sell shares.

Summary of Swing Trading

In this chapter, we have learned the basic techniques of swing trading. The basic idea is that you try and buy shares at a relatively low price. The low price might be the low or support price when the stock is ranging, or it might be a relatively low price that the stock is reaching before going up in a long trend. If the stock is ranging, then you sell your shares when the stock reaches the resistance price. If the stock is in a trend, then you sell your shares when you see that the candlesticks and indicators are showing signs of a trend reversal.

So the goal of swing trading is to take advantage of short term trends in order to make cash profits, that you get by selling off the shares. The time frames can be any that you are comfortable with, that also is long enough for the trends to play out. This can be two days, a week, or several weeks. This depends on the style of the swing trader or on the movement of the stock.

Swing trading can be done on a part-time or full-time basis. Since swing trading is based on longer-term and therefore gradual price changes, it's not necessary to sit at the computer all day long. Many people that engage in swing trading do it only an hour or two a day while keeping their regular jobs. Of course, if you can build it up to that level, you can swing trade full time.

Risk Mitigation when Swing Trading

Swing trading can be a high-risk activity, but you can take some steps to mitigate and minimize your risks. The first thing you want to avoid is losing a lot of money in a trade that doesn't work the way you anticipated. This can be done by placing a stop-loss order, at a level of pricing that indicates the amount of money you are willing to lose on the trade.

Financial advisors, who are a bit of a conservative lot, are going to recommend that you only accept a 2% loss. This means that you are willing to risk 2% of your total account value on a single trade. If you have a $10,000 account, that means you would be willing to risk $200 on a single trade. That might not sound like much, but you spread this amount on a per-share basis.

Let's say that you are trading AMD, which is about $30 a share. If you were to buy $3,000 worth or 100 shares, then you would be able to risk $200/100 = $2 per share.

So the way this would work, is you place a stop-loss order on the trade, set at $28. So if the stock price, which of course you are hoping is going to rise so that you can earn profits, drops to $28 a share instead, the shares will immediately and automatically sell and you will exit the trade. This will protect you from further losses, and at this point, you have only lost $200 from your account. So the losses were minimal. If the stock dropped by a large amount, you would have been protected from further losses.

If you want to, you can study the charts manually in order to look for the best time to sell your shares and earn your profits. Many people get into swing trading because they enjoy studying the charts and doing the analysis, and so they will be happy to engage in this type of activity.

Others, however, may want to enter a take profit order. For example, we can go back to our example of buying shares of AMD at $30 a share. If we are happy with a $3 profit per share and we are expecting the stock to rise to at least this value, then we can put in a take profit order at $33 a share. Remember this is also called a stop-limit order, and so you can place a stop-limit order specifying a price above the current market price and automatically sell your shares if the price goes to this level.

This way you can automate your trading, with the stop loss and stop-limit orders. This is a handy way to mitigate risk if you are someone who is only able to swing trade on a part-time basis. So while you are at work during the day or engaging in other activities, you don't have to sit and watch the markets all day long.

Who is swing trading for?

Swing trading is for anyone who wants to make cash profits off relatively short term movements of stock prices. It is a for-profit business activity. You don't have to set up an official business to do it, it's possible to do swing trading and consider it an individual or sole proprietor activity. But as a swing trader, the point is you are looking to make fast cash, you are not investing. Also, you are not concerned with the companies that you are trading, rather than hoping that they are going to have large price swings that you can earn profits from. The fundamental analysis that we talked about earlier is not of concern to the swing trade. They are not in it for the long term investment.

But the bottom line is that anyone who wants to make money can swing trade. That doesn't mean you will be successful, swing trading is a pretty high-risk activity.

One question people have is can you swing trade and invest for the long term. In fact, you can. Some people have long term investment plans but also swing trade, either to make a living so that they can be all in with the stock market or even to raise funds to invest more in stocks. So you can keep a full-time job, invest in stocks for the long term, and then do swing trading on the side to raise extra money so that you can increase your stock purchases for more long term investing.

Chapter 8: Trader Psychology

In order to be a successful trader, you need to have a trader mindset. In this chapter, we are going to briefly discuss the successful mindset of a trader. It's important to be disciplined as a trader so that you can avoid the pitfalls that suck in novice traders and lead them to large losses.

Don't Let Emotion Rule Your Trades

One of the problems that happen with trading is that emotions can get intense when there are the possibilities of losing or earning a great deal of money over a short time period. This problem also impacts long term investors, who may become fearful of losing their money when they see stock prices collapsing.

In either case, we are talking about people ruling their investments or trades using emotion instead of the logic that is really needed to make good decisions. For traders, you can help get around this by automating your trades, at least to mitigate downside risk. That way you decide ahead of time what the amount of loss you are willing to accept on the trade is, hopefully by using the 2% rule. That rule has been arrived at by financial experts as a result of analyzing large numbers of trades and determining what a safe level of loss is that you can take on a single trade and largely keep your overall brokerage account relatively intact. That way, you are going to be able to live to trade another day, so to speak.

Long term investors often don't have this kind of protection. The reason is that you don't want to be placing stop-loss orders on long term investments, you are hoping to stay in these investments for the long term, after all. And that means that you are going to need to ride out drops in the stock market without panic. But all too often, long term investors – or people that think of themselves as long term investors, give in to the panic and join the other lemmings running off the cliff and they sell their shares. As we've said repeatedly, this is not something that you want to let yourself do. But, since there is no stop-loss order, you can place to prevent it, you are going to have to seek out discipline and avoid doing it using your own mental effort. This can be difficult during a major crash when you are going to see yourself losing a lot of money on paper. Remember that downtrends are buying opportunities, and so you should be buying up stocks instead of selling them.

It's often best to go against the crowd in the stock market, especially when we are talking about small investors.

Traders also need to avoid getting sucked in by greed. In most cases, swing traders are looking at the possibility of making profits from relatively small price movements, and if the price moves to the point at which they need to take profits, but they don't, it can drop 50 cents a share or a dollar a share, and the trader might see the opportunity for profit evaporate. You don't want to hold on too long for profits in a trade, but many traders get overcome by greed and think if they just hold on a little bit longer, they can make big money.

Plan Ahead

This brings us to the next important trader mindset, which is planning. A trader, whether you are a long term investor or some kind of trader like a swing trader, needs to have carefully thought out plans in place that they can use in order to direct their actions when they actually enter a position.

Before entering a trade, a swing trader needs to have the stop loss value for the shares and the take profit value already figured out before you actually buy your shares. A trader who is not planning, and *executing* specific plans are just groping around in the dark. Instead of doing that you should know beforehand what your goals are, and how you are going to reach your goals. You need to have specific ideas as to how much money you are going to make and how much you are hoping to make every week.

Have a trading routine

It's a good idea to have a trading routine. If you are trading full-time, then you want to have a morning routine that you use to start your trading day. This should include paying attention to financial news so that you can get wind of unexpected results that could impact your trades. Sometimes, there are going to be surprised, that means you might need to change your trading plans.

If you are only trading on a part-time basis, then you should still have a routine that you use daily to stay on top of your trades. Maybe you will do this in part on your lunch hour during workdays so that you can make sure that you are keeping up with the progress of your trades and you have the ability to make some adjustments. In addition, you should also have some time either in the early morning hours, or in the evening, or even both if you are able to, where you analyze your trades or study in order to find new trades to enter.

The specifics of your routine are less important than the fact that you either have one, or you don't. Those who don't have a routine are unlikely to be the ones that are successful as swing traders.

Keep Educating Yourself

As a swing trader, you need to recognize that this is a specialized skill. It's not a hobby, it's a professional activity. In order to succeed at any professional activity, you need to keep up with your education and keep honing and improving your skills. So you should study swing trading and the financial markets at every opportunity so that over time you are going to become a better trader.

Maintain a Journal

Traders and investors should keep a trading journal. Enter all your activities related to your trading as if it was a diary. You should also keep a section where you keep a record of your trades, including how much you paid to enter the position and how much you got out of it, including losses if they occur. You should also keep a net running total for each month and for the year. It's important to go on actual recorded information in order to know if you are succeeding or failing at trading, rather than going off the hope of a couple of recent wins and fooling yourself by neglecting to remember the losses that have also occurred.

Don't be impulsive

Next to panic when you are facing losses on a trade or greed when you think you can get more and more money, the worst kind of emotion or action that you can take while trading is making impulsive moves. Unfortunately, being impulsive is very common among novice traders.

Impulsive decisions often result from hyper-excitement. A trader might see a trend or hear some news that in their mind makes a trade a "sure thing." Then without doing any kind of analysis, they enter the trade with no planning, and since there was no analysis done, they can quickly find out that the trade goes the wrong way and works against them instead.

Stick to One Trading Technique

Don't try to be a jack of all trades. So if you want to be a day trader, you should become a day trader. If you want to become a swing trader, then become a swing trader. You shouldn't try being all things at once, even if you hear that others are successful in doing so. Some people can do both styles of trading, while also maintaining long term investments. But most people are not going to find success trying to do everything. Pick one trading style and become an expert at it.

Become an expert on a small number of securities

The market, by its very nature, is volatile. This means that most if not all stocks provide plenty of opportunities to earn money by swing trading. It can help your swing trading if you primarily on a few different stocks. Pick 3-5 to use in order to do your swing trading. Learn the stocks inside and out, so that you know their 52-week highs and lows, and so that you have time to carefully study their charts and look for the right opportunities to enter trades. Having at most five means that you are going to be able to look at the stocks and find good opportunities for swing trading, while not getting overwhelmed. Having at least three ensures that at any given time, you are going to be able to find trades to enter.

Don't be afraid to wait on your trades

As a swing trader, you may be anxious to earn money from your trades, but there is not any rule that says you have to get out of a position before earning the profits that you hope to earn. Unless the stock has crashed down and just isn't going to rebound up to a level where you are able to earn profits, you should be patient and wait long enough for the price to rise to the appropriate pricing level for profits. Unlike day traders, which are high-pressure types that have to act fast, swing trading is a more relaxed and patient trading style. Have the patience to wait overnight, and even weeks if you have to in order to realize your profits.

Don't be afraid to sit on the sidelines

Sometimes, the opportunities to swing trade and earn profits – while still doing the careful analysis – are not going to be there. As a swing trader being anxious is not going to be a helpful characteristic. You are going to want to be able to sit on the sidelines if necessary, waiting for the right trade before you jump into a position. Remember that at the end of the year, your total annual results of wins and losses are what is going to matter. Being constantly in trades is not what matters. So if you have to wait a few days or even a week to find a solid trade that is likely to be a winner, then be prepared to wait. It is better to wait a few days to get into a winning trade than it is to be impulsive and then have your money tied up in less promising or even losing trades, while you see the good trades pass you by.

Chapter 9: Stocks vs. ETFs

In this chapter, we are going to investigate an important topic that is mostly something that needs to be considered for long term investors. And that is whether or not you should invest in stocks or if you should invest in exchange-traded funds, or ETFs, instead. Let's start by understanding what an ETF is for those who are not familiar with the concept.

What is an ETF?

To learn what an ETF is, you start by imagining that there is a large pool of money that you have available for investing. We are talking a large amount that a Wall Street firm might have. They decide to start a fund, which is going to be built by investing in an array of different assets. Then they can sell shares in the fund by dividing it up into small amounts. So in other words, they create shares of stock, but instead of buying stock in a company you are buying stock in the fund.

For the sake of being more specific, let's say that they have $10 million. They decide to create a tech fund, and so they use this $10 million to buy shares in companies like Apple,

Microsoft, IBM, Amazon, Facebook, Intel, and so forth. The fund manager might pick out 20, 50, or 100 stocks to invest in. So they use the $10 million to buy shares in these companies, and then they divide up the $10 million into shares that they start off valued at $50 each. So, there are 200,000 shares available when the fund is initially offered. So you can buy shares in the fund at $50 each, and then as the underlying stocks increase or decrease in value, the share price is going to track them and increase or decrease in value. The fund, of course, will have a life of its own. People who want diversified exposure to these companies are going to be interested in buying shares in the fund, and when these companies are doing well, more people are going to be interested in buying shares, and they will bid up the price of a share in the fund.

There are many different ways that you can construct the fund. You could divide up the shares equally among the different companies in the fund. Alternatively, you could spend an equal amount of money purchasing shares in each company. Another Wall Street firm could buy shares in the same companies so that they could offer a similar fund. But, they might divide or allocate the shares differently among the companies because they think that they have found a better way to build the fund so it will have higher returns.

Wall Street Firm A could allocate the fund as follows:

- 15% invested in Apple
- 10% invested in Facebook
- 8% invested in Microsoft
- 6% invested in IBM

However, Wall Street Firm B might weight things differently, even if they are investing in the same companies:

- 13% in Facebook
- 10% in Apple
- 9% in Amazon
- 7% in IBM
- 5% in Microsoft

Over time, the different weightings may lead one fund to outperform another. In our hypothetical example, we could imagine that Fund A has annual returns of 10%, and Fund B has annual returns of 7%.

These funds will collect dividends, as well. While Apple, Microsoft, and IBM pay dividends, Facebook and Amazon don't. So the fund will collect the dividend money and then divided it up equally among the shares in the fund. In our example, we imagined that there were 200,000 shares. So let's say for the sake of example, that the fund collects $450,000 annually in dividend payments. It then divides up this amount equally among the shares, and so pays $2.50 of its own dividends to the investors in the fund.

Remember that in the chapter on dividends, we mentioned that the manager of an ETF can decide what to do with the dividends. Of course, the fund manager must pay out the dividends in some way to the investors, but they can choose to pay cash to the investors or buy more shares for the investors in the fund on their behalf. Of course if the investors actually want cash and they are given shares instead, they can sell the shares and then take the profits from the sale as a defacto dividend payment.

This is the basic concept of an exchange-tradedfund. There are ETFs for many different sectors, indexes, and even asset classes. So you can invest in bonds, money market funds, or gold, using ETFs. You can also invest in multiple sectors like energy or healthcare. Some of the most popular ETFs that people invest in are index funds. So you can track any major stock market index including the Dow Jones Industrial Average, S & P 500, or the Russell 3000.

Advantages of ETFs

The first major advantage of investing in ETFs is that they give you instant diversification. Not only that, since these funds can invest in hundreds of companies at once, the level of diversification can be described as basically massive. So you are going to have far more diversified exposure using ETFs than you can possibly get investing in individual stocks. As a small investor who does not have the capacity to invest in dozens or hundreds of stocks, going the ETF route can be a distinct advantage.

The second advantage of ETFs is that you can invest in maybe 10 funds, and have exposure across sectors, large-cap, small-cap, and mid-cap companies, asset classes, and different indexes. You can also use ETFs in order to get exposure to overseas markets. This is a major advantage because doing that on an individual basis can be difficult and even problematic. Using ETFs, you let the fund managers and large Wall Street firms handle the difficulties of say investing in Brazil or China for you, while you can sit back with diversified exposure to these high growth markets, helping you to earn significant returns without having to worry about putting your money directly into foreign markets.

Another advantage of ETFs is that due to their natural diversification, they tend to have very high annual returns. It is not uncommon to see ETFs with annual returns of 10-12% over the lifetime of the fund. So if you are an investor who does not want to do a huge amount of fundamental analysis, but you are looking to earn large annual returns to grow your wealth aggressively, then ETFs might be a better option for you.

Of course, you are going to have to do a bit of fundamental analysis on fund investing as well as with individual stocks, but it's a lot less involved. The annual returns, any dividends paid, and the P/E ratios might be the only things that you have to keep track of. There is no pouring over financial statements and that sort of thing.

Remember that the second tactic used when trying to reach your financial goals is dollar-cost averaging. Since you can use ETFs to essentially have automatic diversification, you can concentrate on using dollar-cost averaging to make sure that you are buying into the funds at the best possible average prices.

Bond Investing

Keep in mind that you can invest in almost any asset class there is, using ETFs. But even so, you are investing in stocks. ETFs are stocks that trade on the stock exchanges, and so you are going to have to do research to find the funds that you want to invest in and learn their tickers so that you can buy shares in the funds.

Now, even though ETFs themselves are stocks, they are not required to invest in stocks. They can invest in virtually anything. So you can, for example, do some bond investing indirectly by buying into ETFs that are themselves buying bonds. You will collect the interest payments from these bonds, so this provides another way to earn income from your investments. Bond funds can also see some decent annual returns, even if they are not going to be the best possible investments for that purpose. That said, they are going to be quite competitive. This provides a way to get into corporate, federal, and municipal bonds. There is also the possibility of using ETFs in order to invest in foreign bonds.

Stocks or ETFs? The ultimate question

When it comes to the stock or ETF question, it is not necessarily something that requires you to choose one or the other. In fact, many investors are going to do a little bit of both. But after studying the issue, you might find out that you want to stick with ETFs. There is really good reason to only invest in ETFs, you get high annual returns, massively diversified exposure, and they trade like stocks and so don't suffer from the drawbacks that mutual funds do. You can find virtually any kind of fund to invest in to meet your overall investment goals because fund managers seem to be sitting around all day dreaming up new ways to create competitive and interesting ETFs. Right now, cryptocurrency is probably the only thing that you can't invest in using ETFs, but that will probably change in the near future.

Some people are just attracted to the idea of investing in individual stocks, however. For those readers who want to pursue that path, that is certainly a valid way to engage in long term investing. Presumably, if you are looking to go down that road, this means that you find finance and the markets to be something that you are interested in and so you are willing to put the work in and probably enjoy the fundamental analysis and so forth.

It's also possible to do a mix. Some people who are interested in investing in several individual companies might use ETFs to build some diversity into their investment portfolio. This way, you don't have to worry as much about being diversified when it comes to your stock picks. So you can pick 3-5 companies that you really want to focus on and that you are interested in from an investment perspective, and use some ETFs to ensure you've got the security of diversification working for you at the same time.

Are ETFs better than stock? In most cases, they probably are. Of course, there are a small number of stocks like Amazon or Apple that really grow and can build wealth for you over time. But most stocks are not going to grow to the degree that those companies did. So generally speaking ETFs are going to be better for investors. That can include the fact that they tend to earn very high returns in many cases. They also require very little analysis, and it's easy to move in and out of different funds when you see that your goals are not being met.

In the end, however, it is a personal decision. Each investor is going to have their own tastes and opinions. So you will have to pick which way of investing works best for you and go from there.

Chapter 10: Employee Stock Options and IPOS – What the Stock Trader Won't Tell You

In this chapter, we are going to take a look at some other things you need to know about employee stock options, and also take a look at initial public offerings, or IPOs. IPOs can be important for those with employee stock options if they have stock options at a company that is going to go public at some point. You might also want to learn a bit about IPOs if you are simply looking for investment opportunities.

Types of Employee Stock Options

A company can issue two different types of employee stock options. The first is called an NQs or NSO. This is a non-qualified stock option. If an employee stock option is non-qualified, when you exercise the options, taxes will be withheld at that time. You will have to pay ordinary income tax on the difference in pricing for the shares. What we mean by this is that you are going to have to pay income tax on the difference between the market price of the shares and the grant price of the shares.

Another type of stock option is called an incentive stock option, or ISO. If you can get this type of employee stock option, you are better off. The reason is that rather than paying the ordinary income tax rates, with an ISO you will get to pay the capital gains tax rates. If these are long term capital gains tax rates, then you are going to be in a favorable position tax-wise, paying much lower rates.

IPOs

In many cases, a company that you have employee stock options with may go public, or have an "initial public offering" or IPO. It is important to understand a little bit about IPOs if you are in this situation.

The first thing to understand about IPOs is how the share pricing is set. This is done by auction. A Dutch auction is one where investors place bids to indicate the highest price they are willing to pay for the stock. Then the highest bid is taken after all bids have been placed and used to price the stock. However, there is a different way to conduct a Dutch auction. In this alternative method, the price of the stock is set and then lowered until someone accepts the bid for a sale.

An IPO can also be conducted using what is called traditional allocation. In this case, the minimum price for the stock is determined. Investors who bid the minimum price are then granted shares. This method is considered better for inside holders of stock because the shares are instantly allocated.

When thinking about an IPO, you also need to know about the underwriter. The underwriter is a type of middleman. The underwriter will be an investment bank like Goldman Sachs. They play the role of selling the stock to the initial round of investors, and so they play the role of middleman between the company and the investors.

Chapter 11: Notes on Tax Treatments

As a new investor, it is important that you get some general idea of how investments in the stock market are taxed. This can depend on what you are doing and how long you are investing in. The length of time that you hold an asset can be an important consideration when it comes to the treatment given for taxes. In this chapter, we are going to take a brief look at some of the most important considerations.

Selling Stock

The first situation that we are going to look at is the case of buying the stock at a low price, relatively speaking, and then selling it later for a higher price so that you earn profits. The way that this is treated for tax purposes is as a capital gain. However, the length of time that the shares are held before selling them determines how they are going to be taxed.

If you hold the stock for less than one year, then the profits are taxed as short term capital gains. That means that in short, you are going to be paying ordinary income tax on the gains made from selling the stock while holding it for less than a year. If your income tax rate is 37.3%, then that is what you are going to pay on any profits made from short term stock sales. If your income tax rate is 20%, that is what you will pay.

The bottom line for swing traders is that you are going to pay ordinary income tax rates on all of the profits that you earn as a swing trader.

Long term investors are probably going to pay long term capital gains tax rates. To qualify for long term tax rates, you need to hold an asset for one year or longer. So those who follow the Warren Buffett strategy are going to hold their stocks for many years or decades, before selling them off to earn cash. Then you will pay the long term capital gains taxes on your profits. Under present law, these tax rates are very favorable compared to ordinary income tax rates.

Individual Retirement Accounts (IRAs)

Now let's consider the tax situation with IRAs. If you invest in a traditional IRA, you get the tax benefit now. That means you are able to deduct the money that you invest in the IRA from your current year's taxes. However, when you withdraw the money later, you are going to have to pay ordinary income taxes on your withdrawals. Of course, nobody knows the future, so it's not possible to know if the tax rates today are going to be better or the tax rates in the future are going to be better.

If you have a Roth IRA, then you are going to pay taxes on the investments now. However, when you pull money out of the IRA in the future, the money is going to be tax-free at that point. Again, we don't know what the tax rates are going to be in ten, twenty, or thirty years, so it's really not possible to say that one method is better than the other with any certainty. However, to use a Roth IRA there are limits to the amount of ordinary income that you earn each year, so not everyone is going to be able to use a Roth IRA.

Dividends from REITs, MLPs, and BDCs

Investments in REITs, MLPs, and BDCs pay dividends. These dividends are treated as ordinary income from these companies. However, in the case of a master limited partnership, they are going to pass on their depreciation costs to you. These costs can be quite large, and so generate massive tax savings. You are able to deduct the depreciation costs from your own taxes, and so you will end up paying a very low effective tax rate.

Dividends from Corporations

Dividend payments from ordinary corporations traded on the stock exchanges are treated as qualified dividends if you have held the stock at least 60 days before the payment of the dividends. In that case, they are treated as long term capital gains, and so get the favorable capital gains tax rates. If you held the asset less than 60 days, they are treated as ordinary income.

Chapter 12: Metrics for Value Investors

In this chapter, we are going to review some more metrics that can be used by value investors. You need to understand what all the different metrics are in order to do a fair analysis of the company and determine whether or not it is a good investment for you. We have already discussed doing financial analysis and looking at price to earnings ratio. In this chapter, we will briefly consider some of the more important metrics including price to book ratio, debt ratio, and current ratio.

Price to Book Ratio

The price to book ratio can be an important metric when analyzing the financial health of a company and its long term prospects. The price to book ratio can, like the price to earnings ratio, be something that you can use in order to compare a company to other similar companies in its sector, and also to market averages. This can then help you determine whether or not the company is a value stock or whether it's actually an overpriced stock.

So what is the price to book ratio, and how can we use it to make our investment decisions? Let us have a look.

The price to book ratio is often displayed using the symbol P/B. Here, P is the same value used in the price to earnings ratio. It is simply the current market price of a stock. B is the book value per share. Book value is an accounting term, certain to give many readers headaches. So we won't go into it too deeply, we will only explain that this is a measure of a company's assets less depreciation. This is also called the "carrying value." Or in plain English, it is the net asset value of the company. So they take all of their assets and then subtract liabilities.

If a company has a healthy book value, this is a good sign for the company, but for investors, we are interested in making a comparison of the stock price to the book value. A high value is an indication that the stock may be overpriced.

However, as was the case for the price to earnings ratio, this is not going to be something that you can simply take at face value. You can begin by comparing to stock market averages, and if the company is in an index like the S & P

500, you can also make a comparison to the average value for that index. That said, the really important value that you want to use is making a comparison with other similar companies. So you need to find out what the P/B ratio is for companies that are the closest competitors. Then you want to look at the P/B ratio for the entire sector. If the P/B ratio is low when making these comparisons, then you know that the stock is a value stock, and probably a good buy. But of course, you do not want to do this calculation in isolation. Only a novice investor would buy stock based only on one metric. You should also check the P/E ratio to determine if the company is a value stock or not. The P/B ratio helps you determine the value of the company in terms of its net assets. This is different than P/E, which helps you determine the value of the stock in terms of company earnings. Both are important, but frankly, the P/E ratio is probably more important when trying to determine if we are talking about a value stock or not.

Debt and Current Ratios

The debt and current ratios are two more metrics that we can use in order to evaluate the financial state of a company. When doing value investing, you are going to be looking for companies that are in good financial health, and so what you want to see is these companies are not taking on too much debt.

The debt ratio takes the total debt and divides it by the total value of the assets of the company. This is a red flag if the debt ratio is greater than 1.0. What the debt ratio tells you is how much ability the company has to pay off its debts. Obviously, a company is not going to have a fire sale and get rid of all its assets in order to pay the debt, but you want to have some measure of how much the debt really impacts the company. A company may have a lot of debt in absolute terms, but if it has even more assets, then that debt is not necessarily a dangerous or bad thing for the company. The debt ratio gives you an idea of how able the company is to pay off its long term debt obligations or put another way its total debt.

We are also interested in how able the company is to pay off its short term debt obligations that are due in less than one year. This information comes from the current ratio. This found from the balance sheet, you want to get current debt/liabilities and compare that to assets. Again, the lower the ratio the better when it comes to debts. If the company has a lot going for it, taking on debt is not necessarily a bad thing. For example, a company may be developing important and exciting products for the future that may bring in lots of revenues.

Conclusion

Thank you for taking the time to read this book.

I hope that the information presented in this book has opened new doors for you, showing you the many possibilities that exist to build your own wealth doing self-directed investing. It is far easier than most people think, and you can build up your own portfolio of stocks to generate wealth now and in the future.

We also hoped to impress upon the reader the importance of not bypassing the opportunities that stock options from an employer can offer. Many people would prefer to take cash, but stock options offer the opportunity to grow wealth over time, which is more important over the long run. We also covered some of the details of employee stock options, so that you can better know how to handle them and whether that is the right thing for your situation.

We've also learned about the opportunities that exchange-traded fund investing provides, and how this compares and contrasts with investing in individual stocks. You should do what is best for your own situation, but most readers will probably benefit from doing a mix of the two investment styles.

Most of all, we have learned the promise of value investing that is promoted by successful investors like Warren Buffett. By following a clear and disciplined investment strategy, anyone can build massive amounts of wealth. It does take time, so there is no time like now to get started!

We also covered many of the important characteristics of a stock that investors should be looking at. These include the many metrics that will tell you at a glance what the health of a given company is so that you can determine whether or not investing in that company is going to be something that you want to do in order to secure your own financial future. Next, we discussed the opportunities that are presented by IPOs and what to look for when considering this as a possible move for your portfolio. This may not be something you are looking at right now, but in the future you may find this to be an opportunity to further grow your wealth.

Finally, we discussed the tax implications of investing in the stock market.

Thank you again for making it all the way through my book, and please leave an Amazon review with your thoughts.

Disclaimer

Please note that *Stock Option Trading*, Jim Livermore, and anyone related to creating this book are not to be held liable for any results that the reader may gain from trading using these strategies. This book is designed for educational purposes only and should be viewed as such by the reader. Any action the reader takes on the information in this book is solely the responsibility and liability of the reader themselves, no one else.

My FREE Gift for You

If you buy my other title, *"Stock Option Trading Strategies"* I will give you the 2 *"Stock Option Trading"* Audiobooks 100% FREE! Stock Option Trading Strategies is an excellent title that teaches you all about this trading sector. In that book we are going to reveal all the secrets about options, and how professional options traders are able to make money month-to-month and even build up wealth over time. Can you imagine having a life of financial freedom where you are in control of your life and not having to answer to any boss? This is possible using options trading – but you have to know the right way to go about it.

What Should I Read Next?

Swing Trading for Beginners: The 2019/20 Valuable Swing Trading Guide for Learning How to Improve Your Trading Results and Your Finances with the Best Low-Risk Approaches

Swing Trading Option: The Ultimate Trading Guide to Discover Safe and Profitable Trading Strategies for Generating Fast and Secure Profits and Rapid Growth for Your Finances

Stock Options Trading Strategies: The Best Step-by-Step Guide to Learn How to Trade Stocks and Discover How TOP Traders Invest. The Best Strategies to Help You Create Your Financial Freedom

Options Trading: The Best Beginner's Guide with All the Essential Information an Investor Needs on How the Options Market Works and How to Start Trading Options in 2019/2020.

Forex trading strategy: How to Invest with the Most Profitable and Simple Strategies to Make Money Trading Stocks, Options, Forex, Etfs in 2019 / 2020 Working Just 30 Minutes per Day.

www.ingramcontent.com/pod-product-compliance
Lightning Source LLC
Chambersburg PA
CBHW070338220526
45467CB00001B/162